# Canadian Poetry

# The Modern Era

# Canadian Poetry

## The Modern Era

### Edited by John Newlove

McCLELLAND AND STEWART

© 1977 by McClelland and Stewart Limited

ALL RIGHTS RESERVED

ISBN: 0-7710-6731-3

*The Canadian Publishers*
McClelland and Stewart Limited
25 Hollinger Road, Toronto

Printed and bound in Canada

Canadian Cataloguing in Publication Data

Main entry under title:

Canadian poetry

Bibliography: p.
ISBN 0-7710-6731-3

1. Canadian poetry (English) - 20th century.*
I. Newlove, John, 1938-

PS8273.C35      C811'.5'408      C77-001061-X
PR9195.7.C35

# Contents

## A. M. KLEIN

## IRVING LAYTON

## DENNIS LEE

## DOROTHY LIVESAY

## RAYMOND SOUSTER

## MIRIAM WADDINGTON

# PREFACE

This selection is based on a survey done of the needs of Canadian literature instructors in universities across the country. They were asked which modern Canadian poets ("modern" meaning, roughly, those writing from 1945 to the present, with a few exceptions) should be represented in an anthology, and to what degree. The response was overwhelming. From this, it was possible to sketch out the size, form, and content of the book.

I am grateful for this help. When the area of choice is so rich a one as modern Canadian poetry in English, the making of an anthology becomes a matter of leaving things out rather than of putting things in.

I have read some thousands of poems over the past two years. Certain distinctions became arbitrary. To cite the most obvious: concrete poetry is not represented; in general, the longer poem has been omitted for reasons of space and because I did not wish to excerpt, although I occasionally had to do so; when I had a decision between two of a poet's works, I generally took the one less anthologized. I have tried to be practical.

Readers (and reviewers) of anthologies must necessarily compare them to that ideal list they themselves would have compiled, so that no other's effort is ever completely satisfactory. For myself, confronted with so many choices, I decided to assemble a book that was both a survey and a source, and one that could be read with pleasure. (This is an emotion sometimes neglected in poetry today.) To that end, though there is a short bibliography and though short biographical notes, often supplied by the poets, are included, I have preserved as much space as possible for the actual poems.

Whenever it was possible, I have consulted the poets and they have been immensely helpful. In several cases, the poets revised earlier work, so that we have the definitive versions here. Peter Saunders and Peter Milroy germinated the project and prodded and encouraged me for two years, and Gerda West has done more in the practical making of this book than I can ever thank her for.

# MILTON ACORN

## IN MEMORY OF TOMMY, AN ORPHAN, WHO WAS KIDNAPPED FROM HIS LOVING FOSTER-MOTHER, KATHERINE, IN FULFILLMENT OF A BARGAIN BETWEEN CHURCHES

No wonder the boy dreamt of monsters
terrible in horns, mooing his name,
chasing to tickle and eat him; no wonder
these drownpools of eyes looked in
the second storey window, their bland face
brooding cruel grown-up abstractions;
no wonder that dinosaur with the cooing
dove voice, too big to hide in a barn:
no wonder he woke with terror caught
like a fishbone in his throat, to huddle
amidst a dark full of faces.

I don't know if hate's the armour of love;
what side he joined, or if he joined: but
when he learned to hate those dreams ended.

## THE ISLAND

Since I'm Island-born home's as precise
as if a mumbly old carpenter,
shoulder-straps crossed wrong,
laid it out,
refigured to the last three-eighths of shingle.

Nowhere that plow-cut worms
heal themselves in red loam;
spruces squat, skirts in sand;
or the stones of a river rattle its dark
tunnel under the elms,
is there a spot not measured by hands;
no direction I couldn't walk
to the wave-lined edge of home.

In the fanged jaws of the Gulf,
a red tongue.
Indians say a musical God
took up his brush and painted it;
named it, in His own language,
"The Island."

# SKY'S POEM FOR CHRISTMAS

As from milky vapour, dust of atoms jostling like hornets,
a nebula swigs great swatches of itself into a new sun
raw with light, ravener to its parent mists, messenger
to far astronomers thirsty for the word, the word
that'll unlock them: I've never lost a faith
or wrenched my roots of eyes from the heart. . . .
Each doom to joy and torment's nourished
within an old love, becomes a new focus
pulsing radiation, disrupting
the foggy smut of death about it;
while I still step to the blood's rhythm,
the soul's reason in those old stories
of kings and white-hot new stars, wonderful babes
like Jupiter's yowl making that Island cave boom like an organ,
born to laugh a challenge at the old cruel gods.

Surely at least once when a new star burst thru heaven
three old men forsook the stern fantasies
of mummy-clothes they'd wrapped around the world,
and surely they found at least one babe
who held great bear time by its short tail. . . .
For birth by birth the many-colored creatures of Earth
break ranks and dance apart calling their names and numbers
to reassemble with shoutings and elbow-digs
in formations first seen by the mindseye of a child.

Christmas I became that ho-ho-ho of a saint
to wind on a balky piebald disbelieving burro
along the Wisemen's trail thru a desert of grown-up people
like cactus with its growth stalled in tormented poses:
til housed and run around by squirrels I found the boy Sky
with eyes hazel windows into outré dimensions
now looking out on wonder, now looking in
at wonder. . . . I came not with gifts but
for a present of the universe made strange, tumbling
with odd fuzzy animals, blue of high heaven
siphoned down to tank up my brain,
for meteors he caught and sent sizzling past my ears:
and for myself made quaint, totemic
like a thick oak come wobbling, walking
grotesquely on its roots over patches of dark and sunlight.

# BETHUNIVERSE

Does a man three decades dead walk and make facial expressions
Among us? When we're shaving do our eyes stray from
   the mirror
And suddenly in vision's discarded corner
Do we see his face? Surely there's a reasonable explanation. . . .

A strong old man gets on the elevator. He
Even has a red sweatshirt – tam tilted at that old angle.
If I could see his eyes I'd know;
But his eyes are screwed shut
                  as if in anguish:

Like many eyes – opening, closing – record anguish. . . .
One sees him again; in many sizes; at many ages;
Suddenly I realize there are many Bethunes.
From many candidates, fate chooses
Both its victims and its heroes
Often one and the same. . . .
Another necessity, another Canuck, and there could have
   been another Bethune.

So many of us live in anguish
Because we were spared his anguish. . . .

Let there be a Bethune Oath
Improving on that of Hippocrates
To make curing no routine but wars against disease;
Strengthen health, increase and lead it
Into all which must be done, all which must be felt, meant
   and seen.

What are we doing? Brave Canucks:
After four hundred years still a colony?
Supplying the basic armstuffs
To conquer a world which includes us?
Since one of us swerved time from its course
There's been no rest.
            Why call it peace?

# RIDING WITH JOE HENSBY

Riding with Joe Hensby in a ten-speed trailer
Down 401 the cab so high we're on a flying throne;
No need to worry of traffic, it worries of you ...
The jungle trails clear when the elephant comes.

Thirty tons of steel behind, fifty miles an hour:
No need to worry – if we got stopped sudden
And all that metal came crashing through
You could spread us on a sandwich and we'd never know.

He plays the gears like a man at a piano
Cursing every time – two or three seconds apart;
At no one in particular
He lives the road ... he lives the abstract world of his curses.
Sometimes I come into his consciousness, but no one else.

But when that stream of vehicles clogs, we slow:
 sitting up there like conjoint kings
One of us's got to point a moral; and I
The official poet: –
 "Jesus Christ Joe
There's ten million dollars of equipment in sight
 – how is it that we're poor?"

Call it a machine, call it a beast, call it a kind of a hand
For it becomes an extension of the man.
When it roars it's we together are the lion:
And we live like lions
 often moving, often waiting
 years to pounce.

# HO CHI MINH

... and still there is the final murderer;
men can't be women, or women men –
we can't be children again
if we were ever children;
nor can the dead become the living. . . .

Imperialists, factionaries, gangsters
felt his heartbeats like beewingbeats
shaking their tailored hates, the rigidities of their minds. . . .
Made plots when they only had to wait.
Such victories are guaranteed.

The child whimpering to silence
in ruins, the aborted baby;
these are, in their ways, greater losses:
for who can tell that sort of probability
and possibilities even greater?
but we knew this one
and his strength was ours. . . .

To be like him? It
would be wrong to be like him;
only in certain things, chosen
and learned with equal bitterness, in later times.
Only he could be himself.

We shall never have this sword again:
We will always need it;
even when, instead of 'sword'
we may say 'flower'.

# MARGARET ATWOOD

## JOURNEY TO THE INTERIOR

There are similarities
I notice: that the hills
which the eyes make flat as a wall, welded
together, open as I move
to let me through; become
endless as prairies; that the trees
grow spindly, have their roots
often in swamps; that this is a poor country;
that a cliff is not known
as rough except by hand, and is
therefore inaccessible. Mostly
that travel is not the easy going
from point to point, a dotted
line on a map, location
plotted on a square surface
but that I move surrounded by a tangle
of branches, a net of air and alternate
light and dark, at all times;
that there are no destinations
apart from this.

There are differences
of course: the lack of reliable charts;
more important, the distraction of small details:
your shoe among the brambles under the chair
where it shouldn't be; lucent
white mushrooms and a paring knife
on the kitchen table; a sentence
crossing my path, sodden as a fallen log
I'm sure I passed yesterday
                              (have I been
walking in circles again?)

but mostly the danger:
many have been here, but only
some have returned safely.

A compass is useless; also
trying to take directions
from the movements of the sun,
which are erratic;
and words here are as pointless
as calling in a vacant
wilderness.
                    Whatever I do I must
keep my head. I know
it is easier for me to lose my way
forever here, than in other landscapes


## THE SETTLERS


A second after
the first boat touched the shore,
there was a quick skirmish
brief as a twinge
and then the land was settled

(of course there was really
no shore: the water turned
to land by having
objects in it: caught and kept
from surge, made
less than immense
by networks of
roads and grids of fences)

and as for us, who drifted
picked by the sharks
during so many bluegreen
centuries before they came:
they found us
inland, stranded
on a ridge of bedrock,
defining our own island.

From our inarticulate
skeleton (so
intermixed, one
carcass),
they postulated wolves.

They dug us down
into the solid granite
where our bones grew flesh again,
came up trees and
grass.

Still
we are the salt
seas that uphold these lands.

Now horses graze
inside this fence of ribs, and

children run, with green
smiles, (not knowing
where) across
the fields of our open hands.

# THE ANIMALS IN THAT COUNTRY

In that country the animals
have the faces of people:

the ceremonial
cats possessing the streets

the fox run
politely to earth, the huntsmen
standing around him, fixed
in their tapestry of manners

the bull, embroidered
with blood and given
an elegant death, trumpets, his name
stamped on him, heraldic brand
because

(when he rolled
on the sand, sword in his heart, the teeth
in his blue mouth were human)

he is really a man

even the wolves, holding resonant
conversations in their
forests thickened with legend.

     In this country the animals
     have the faces of
     animals.

     Their eyes
     flash once in car headlights
     and are gone.

     Their deaths are not elegant.

     They have the faces of
     no-one.

# CHRONOLOGY

I was born senile and gigantic
my wrinkles charting
in pink the heights and ruts, events
of all possible experience.

At 6 I was sly as a weasel,
adroit at smiling and hiding,
slippery-fingered, greasy with guile.

At 12, instructed
by the comicbooks already
latent in my head, I was bored with horror.

At 16 I was pragmatic,
armoured with wry lipstick;
I was invulnerable,
I wore my hair like a helmet.

But by 20 I had begun
to shed knowledge like petals
or scales; and today I discovered
that I have been living backwards.

Time wears me down like water.
The engraved lines of my features
are being slowly expunged.

I will have to pretend:
the snail knows
thin skin is no protection;

though I can't go on
indefinitely. At 50 they will peel
my face away like a nylon stocking

uncovering such incredible blank
innocence, that even mirrors
accustomed to grotesques
will be astounded.

I will be unshelled, I will be
of no use to that city
and like a horse with a broken back
I will have to be taken out and shot.


## PROCEDURES FOR UNDERGROUND
*(Northwest Coast)*


The country beneath
the earth has a green sun
and the rivers flow backwards;

the trees and rocks are the same
as they are here, but shifted.
Those who live there are always hungry;

from them you can learn
wisdom and great power,
if you can descend and return safely.

You must look for tunnels, animal
burrows or the cave in the sea
guarded by the stone man;

when you are down you will find
those who were once your friends
but they will be changed and dangerous.

Resist them, be careful
never to eat their food.
Afterwards, if you live, you will be able

to see them when they prowl as winds,
as thin sounds in our village. You will
tell us their names, what they want, who

has made them angry by forgetting them.
For this gift, as for all gifts, you must
suffer: those from the underland

will be always with you, whispering their
complaints, beckoning you
back down; while among us here

you will walk wrapped in an invisible
cloak. Few will seek your help
with love, none without fear.


## DREAMS OF THE ANIMALS


Mostly the animals dream
of other animals    each
according to its kind

                (though certain mice and small rodents
                have nightmares of a huge pink
                shape with five claws descending)

: moles dream of darkness and delicate
mole smells

frogs dream of green and golden
frogs
sparkling like wet suns
among the lilies

red and black
striped fish, their eyes open
have red and black striped
dreams   defence, attack, meaningful
patterns

birds dream of territories
enclosed by singing.

Sometimes the animals dream of evil
in the form of soap and metal
but mostly the animals dream
of other animals.

There are exceptions:

> the silver fox in the roadside zoo
> dreams of digging out
> and of baby foxes, their necks bitten
>
> the caged armadillo
> near the train
> station, which runs
> all day in figure eights
> its piglet feet pattering,
> no longer dreams
> but is insane when waking;
>
> the iguana
> in the petshop window on St Catherine Street
> crested, royal-eyed, ruling
> its kingdom of water-dish and sawdust
>
> dreams of sawdust.

# THEY EAT OUT

In restaurants we argue
over which of us will pay for your funeral

though the real question is
whether or not I will make you immortal.

At the moment only I
can do it and so

I raise the magic fork
over the plate of beef fried rice

and plunge it into your heart.
There is a faint pop, a sizzle

and through your own split head
you rise up glowing;

the ceiling opens
a voice sings Love Is A Many

Splendoured Thing
you hang suspended above the city

in blue tights and a red cape,
your eyes flashing in unison.

The other diners regard you
some with awe, some only with boredom:

they cannot decide if you are a new weapon
or only a new advertisement.

As for me, I continue eating;
I liked you better the way you were,
but you were always ambitious.

## YOU REFUSE TO OWN

You refuse to own
yourself, you permit
others to do it for you:

you become slowly more public,
in a year there will be nothing left
of you but a megaphone

or you will descend through the roof
with the spurious authority of a
government official,
blue as a policeman, grey as a used angel,
having long forgotten the difference
between an annunciation and a parking ticket

or you will be slipped under
the door, your skin furred with cancelled
airmail stamps, your kiss no longer literature
but fine print, a set of instructions.

If you deny these uniforms
and choose to repossess
yourself, your future

will be less dignified, more painful, death will be sooner,
(it is no longer possible
to be both human and alive): lying piled with
the others, your face and body
covered so thickly with scars
only the eyes show through.

# THERE IS ONLY ONE OF EVERYTHING

Not a tree but the tree
we saw, it will never exist, split by the wind
                              and bending down
like that again. What will push out of the earth

later, making it summer, will not be
grass, leaves, repetition, there will
have to be other words. When my

eyes close language vanishes. The cat
with the divided face, half black half orange
nests in my scruffy fur coat, I drink tea,

fingers curved around the cup, impossible
to duplicate these flavours. The table
and freak plates glow softly, consuming themselves,

I look out at you and you occur
in this winter kitchen, random as trees or sentences,
entering me, fading like them, in time you will disappear

but the way you dance by yourself
on the tile floor to a worn song, flat and mournful,
so delighted, spoon waved in one hand, wisps of
                              roughened hair

sticking up from your head, it's your surprised
body, pleasure I like. I can even say it,
though only once and it won't

last: I want this. I want
this.

# MARGARET AVISON

## JONATHAN, O JONATHAN

The spokes of sun
have pronged and spun:
a bowling barrow – paddle-wheel – or rein
held taut. Careening
early this morning
shod hooves flaked the loose tiles. Sky opened. Horning
farness flooded through.
The high-swivelling blue,
the wet-clay cumulus, and the rough fleur-de-lys
fringeing it, ensource
an unroofed universe,
lettuce-cool largeness. The wrenched miles swing and course,
rivers of speed.
The oven-bread
of earth smokes rainbows. Blind stars and swallows parade
the windy sky of streets
and cheering beats
down faintly, to leaves in sticks, insects in pleats
and pouches hidden
and micro-garden.
At the kitchen-door of their forwardfold backslidden
munching wishes, men,
shouting and toppling
smokestacks like Saturday children, suddenly crane
for the still Make-wish.
Where the roofs slope and flash
are hearts pungent and herbal for the sungold wheels to crush.

# WATERSHED

The world doesn't crumble apart.
The general, and rewarding, illusion
Prevents it. You know what you know in your heart
But there is no traffic in that direction,
Only acres of stained quicksand,
   Stained by the sun
That lingers still at a Muscovite level, ignoring
The clocks in the wrists and the temples, and up in the
    towers
That you see as you walk, assuming the earth your floor
Though you know in your heart that the foot-hold really
    is gone.

(I saw you come out of the painted grove, my buck,
With the bruise of leaf-wet under your eyes,
    In a shy terrible blaze.
  The painted grove, hung stiffly with cold wax
  and fading pigments, issued you complete
And tissued then in myriad light-spots, swivelling
into sheerest space. It was bright and spacious and neat
With everything moving, pricking from points of clear:
    Day-bourne.)

There is a change in the air:
The rain and the dark and the bare
Bunched trees, in pewter fresco, square
From the window. Yes, and you know
In your heart what chill winds blow.
And the clocks in the temples, in all the towers, sound on
(Quarter and half), and the gutters flow, and the sour
Rain pastes the leather-black streets with large pale leaves.

## SEPTEMBER STREET

Harvest apples lack tartness.
The youngest child stares at the brick school wall.
After the surprising *coup* at a late luncheon meeting
    the young man shifting for green concludes
the future makes his bitten thumb the fake.
    A convalescent steps around
wet leaves, resolving on the post-box corner.
    Next time, the young man glimpses,
he will be one of three, not the lone fourth
        susceptible to elation.
    *Yellow.* The pride saddens him.
A van grinds past. Somebody with
considerable dash and a strong left hand
plays Annie Laurie on an untuned piano.
        Granada will not rhyme with Canada.
    The home-grown wines have sharpness.
    A scissor-grinder used to come
    about the hour the school let out
    and children knocked down chestnuts.
        On the yellow porch
    one sits, not reading headlines; the old eyes
        read far out into the mild
            air, runes.
    See. There: a stray sea-gull.

# TWILIGHT

Three minutes ago it was almost dark.
Now all the darkness is in the
leaves (there are no more
low garage roofs, etc.).

But the sky itself has become mauve.
Yet it is raining.
The trees rustle and tap with rain.
. . .Yet the sun is gone.
It would even be gone from the mountaintops
if there were mountains.

In cities this mauve sky
may be of man.

The taps listen, in the unlighted bathroom.

Perfume of light.

It is gone. It is all over:
until the hills close to behind
the ultimate straggler, it will
never
be so again.

The insect of thought retracts its claws;
it wilts.

## JULY MAN

Old, rain-wrinkled, time-soiled, city-wise, morning man
whose weeping is for the dust of the elm-flowers
and the hurting motes of time,
rotted with rotting grape,
sweet with the fumes,
puzzled for good by fermented potato-
peel out of the vat of the times,
turned out and left
in this grass-patch, this city-gardener's place
under the buzzing populace's
square shadows, and the green shadows
of elm and ginkgo and lime
(planted for Sunday strollers and summer evening
families, and for those
bird-cranks with bread-crumbs
and crumpled umbrellas who come
while the dew is wet on the park, and beauty
is fan-tailed, gray and dove gray, aslant, folding in
from the white fury of day).

In the sound of the fountain
you rest, at the cinder-rim, on your bench.

The rushing river of cars
makes you a stillness, a pivot, a heart-stopping
blurt, in the sorrow
of the last rubbydub swig, the searing, and
stone-jar solitude lost, and yet,
and still – wonder (for good now) and
trembling:

> The too much none of us knows
> is weight, sudden sunlight, falling
> on your hands and arms, in your lap,
> all, all, in time.

# WORDS

Heraldry is breath-clouded brass,
blood-rusted silks, gold-pricked even threadbare
memorials of honor
worn,
a shield when napalm and germ-caps and fission are
eyeless towards color, bars, quarterings.

A herald blares in a daybreaking
glory, or foolishly carols –
robin under a green sky – or, a
green earth-breaking tip, is still
but with bodily stillness, not the
enemy's voicelessness.

The ancient, the new,
confused in speech,
breathe on, involving
heart-warmed lungs, the reflexes
of uvula, shaping tongue, teeth, lips,
ink, eyes, and de-
ciphering heart.

# THE ABSORBED

The sun has not absorbed
this icy day, and this day's industry – in
behind glass – hasn't the blue and gold, cold
outside. Though not absorbing, this
sought that:

    sheeted, steely, vaulted,
    all gleam, this morning;
    bright blue with one stained wing in the
        northeast, at lunch hour;
    in early afternoon
    abruptly a dust-flurry,
        all but this private coign of place
        deafened, all winding in one cloth of moth.
    Then space breathed, hollowing twilight
        on ice and the pale-gray, pale-blue,
        and far fur-colored wooden trees
        and ornamental trees.

Towards sundown
a boy came with an aluminum toboggan.
He worked his way, absorbed,
past footmark pocks, on crust,
up ice-ridge, sometimes bumping
down to the Japanese yews, sometimes
scooter-shoving athwart the hill,
then, with a stake,
kneeling,
he paddles, thrusting, speed-wise, then
stabbing, uphill; then
dangling the rope and poring on
slope-sheen, standing, he stashes
the aluminum, upright, in a frost-lumpy shoal
and beside coasting motorcars and parked cars
listens . . . and off again, toque to the eyebrows,
alone still in the engulfing dark.

The inside breathing here
closes down all the window but a visor-slit
on the night glare.

New cold is
in dry-thorn nostrils.

Alone, he plays, still there. We
struggle, our animal fires
pitted against those
several grape-white stars,
their silence.


## MINIATURE BIOGRAPHY OF ONE OF MY FATHER'S FRIENDS WHO DIED A GENERATION AGO


You, sovereign, Lord, have let this be,
Love's gesture here on earth to me.

Your touch would prove all.
Shall I fear it, who want your approval?

My friend's sorrow
I cannot endure. Our
shrinking is your pain.

Let Love's word speak plain.

# FIVE BREAKS

## I

Top-spun, swiftly
paid out,
you flung me, dancing, humming:
    "Joy it is
    to ride the day,
    lest that one toy with
    God's play."
The stranger motif here
stunned my now dizzying ear,
and stilled, I lay
toppled and listening.

## II

No-one at slack but
jerking guy-ropes or (Look out!)
lash-tackle will
entangle.
Rope-burned, wind-sifted,
praising the Stranger courage and
barrenlands beauty,
strong in your buffeting, I
stood, speed-blind, among
your synchronizing glories.

## III

O, then, a careful face
shone bare. In your
held breath, new pinpointed –
were they besiegers' eye-prongs circling
as though a City's famine could be succulence?
I swellingly knew
the aliens, close: all the
my-minded versions of your glory

(like seeing death, life, as your
memoranda left on the blotter
for my day's work; like
chronologies – of "mercies" – these,
these, as if exacted; like
feeling the flesh as tomb
stoned by its own
funereal pieties,
braced for rotting geologies of endurance –
and after that for grubbing,
engine-heat, the
firebird cycle . . . .)

IV

Valentine cards
In the February lace of daylight
through window and doorway glass:
store; children; love; a lakeblue sudsbright
eleven o'clock outdoors, seen too
by the scorched eyes of grief,
the graveled eyes of
utter disappointment, these
zero in the
arrowing sunburst, cone-tip, the
transfixing life.

V

Your tireless rise, your daybreak,
o, here, touch home.

## THE DUMBFOUNDING

When you walked here,
took skin, muscle, hair,
eyes, larynx, we
withheld all honor: "His house is clay,
how can he tell us of his far country?"

Your not familiar pace
in flesh, across the waves,
woke only our distrust.
Twice-torn we cried "A ghost"
and only on our planks counted you fast.

Dust wet with your spittle
cleared mortal trouble.
We called you a blasphemer,
a devil-tamer.

The evening you spoke of going away
we could not stay.
All legions massed. You had to wash, and rise,
alone, and face
out of the light, for us.

You died.
We said,
"The worst is true, our bliss
has come to this."

When you were seen by men
in holy flesh again
we hoped so despairingly for such report
we closed their windpipes for it.

Now you have sought
and seek, in all our ways, all thoughts,
streets, musics – and we make of these a din
trying to lock you out, or in,
to be intent. And dying.

Yet you are
constant and sure,
the all-lovely, all-men's-way
to that far country.

Winning one, you again
all ways would begin
life: to make new
flesh, to empower
the weak in nature
to restore
or stay the sufferer;

lead through the garden to
trash, rubble, hill,
where, the outcast's outcast, you
sound dark's uttermost, strangely light-brimming, until
time be full.


## IN EPORPHYRIAL HARNESS


Hill-hoe
till the liberal varnish, the
daze-sun go
down and the pin-
        flare-
        finish
      star-bright
become alltoday, furnish
us sun (eyes) (ice).

# NATURAL/UNNATURAL

Evening tilt makes a
pencil-box of our
street.
The lake, in largeness, grapey blueness
casts back the biscuit-colored pencil-box, boxes, toys, the
steeple-people, all of it, in one of those
little mirrory shrugs.

The north-east sky too
grows fuselage cool.

On the horizon
ghosts of peeled parsnips point their
noseless faces up,
out; ghost-bodies pile up on each other, all prone, all
pointless, blanking, refusing.

Even the west, beyond the tinged rooftops
smells of cobalt;

     "no – the
     charring of a peeled stick in a bonfire
     is the smell: newness,
      October crackling . . ."
large pink children have, all the same, sniffed
the ice in
that quirk of sunset
but refuse
fear.

There is still a lingering
sand-edge of sound
darkness explores.

In hope I say: it is a
listening into a
voice-sound, a voice making with silence.

"Hope is a dark place
that does not refuse
fear?"

      True, the natural night is pressure on my ribs:
      despair – to draw that in, to
      deflate the skin-pouch, crunch out the
      structure in one
      luxuriant deep-breathed zero –
      dreamed already, this is
      corruption.

I fear *that.*

I refuse, fearing; in hope.

# EARLE BIRNEY

## THIS PAGE MY PIGEON
*(for esther)*


This page is my pigeon sailing
out of the blasted Now to you
my greenest past    my rivered future
See    round his leg snug    love's cylinder

come from this world of wild undoing
from all this quarrel of iron and growth
Weaving by snake-spit of ack-ack and robot's
roar-horror    up past the beautiful brutal

bombers floating like flakes of mica
leaps my faithful feathered one    soars
through the haired and dirty clouds of the war
cleaving cleanly the selfcentered sky

Under apathetic suns and over
the pointless ocean he arrows    off
to the one unlosable loft
What does he say for me    what brings my homer?

Says that your voice still waters my memory
your eyes are leads to the wide light
that will be    Swears you are part of the rightness
of hills    the saneness of music and hemlocks

Says the giraffish dockweed    loneliness
was lopped away long ago    burned in your vaulting fire
when first you gardened me    Now this gyring
windstorm of absence whirls ashes up only

Windseed is barren    takes no truehold
in heart tendrilled tight with existence of you

*Portsmouth 1944*

# ATLANTIC DOOR

Through or over the deathless feud
of the cobra sea and the mongoose wind
you must fare to reach us
through hiss and throttle come
where the great ships are scattered twigs
on a green commotion
where the plane is a fugitive mote
in the stare of the sun
Come by a limbo of motion humbled
under cliffs of cloud
and over gargantuan whalehalls
In this lymph's abyss a billion
years of spawning and dying have passed
and will pass without ministration of man
For all the red infusions of sailors
veins of vikings lost and matelots
haemoglobin of Gilbert's hearties and Jellicoe's
for all blood seeping from corvette and sealer
from sodden hulls of *Hood* and *Titanic*
still do these waves when the gale snaps them
fracture white as the narwhal's tusk
Come then trailing whatever pattern
of gain or solace and think no more than you must
of the simple unhuman truth of this emptiness
that down deep below the lowest pulsing
of primal cell
tar-dark and dead
lie the bleak and forever capacious tombs of the sea

*Grand Banks 1945*

# FROM THE HAZEL BOUGH

I met a lady
        on a lazy street
hazel eyes
        and little plush feet

her legs swam by
        like lovely trout
eyes were trees
        where boys leant out

hands in the dark and
        a river side
round breasts rising
        with the finger's tide

she was plump as a finch
        and live as a salmon
gay as silk and
        proud as a Brahmin

we winked when we met
        and laughed when we parted
never took time
        to be brokenhearted

but no man sees
        where the trout lie now
or what leans out
        from the hazel bough

*Military Hospital, Toronto 1945/Vancouver 1947*

## BUSHED

He invented a rainbow but lightning struck it
shattered it into the lake-lap of a mountain
so big his mind slowed when he looked at it

Yet he built a shack on the shore
learned to roast porcupine belly and
wore the quills on his hatband

At first he was out with the dawn
whether it yellowed bright as wood-columbine
or was only a fuzzed moth in a flannel of storm
But he found the mountain was clearly alive
sent messages whizzing down every hot morning
boomed proclamations at noon and spread out
a white guard of goat
before falling asleep on its feet at sundown

When he tried his eyes on the lake    ospreys
would fall like valkyries
choosing the cut-throat
He took then to waiting
till the night smoke rose from the boil of the sunset

But the moon carved unknown totems
out of the lakeshore
owls in the beardusky woods derided him
moosehorned cedars circled his swamps and tossed
their antlers up to the stars
then he knew    though the mountain slept    the winds
were shaping its peak to an arrowhead
poised

And now he could only
bar himself in and wait
for the great flint to come singing into his heart

*Wreck Beach 1951*

# EL GRECO: *ESPOLIO*


The carpenter is intent on the pressure of his hand

on the awl   and the trick of pinpointing his strength
through the awl to the wood   which is tough
He has no effort to spare for despoilings
or to worry if he'll be cut in on the dice
His skill is vital to the scene   and the safety of the state
Anyone can perform the indignities   It's his hard arms
and craft that hold the eyes of the convict's women
There is the problem of getting the holes exact
(in the middle of this elbowing crowd)
and deep enough to hold the spikes
after they've sunk through those bared feet
and inadequate wrists he knows are waiting behind him.

He doesn't sense perhaps that one of the hands
is held in a curious gesture over him –
giving or asking   forgiveness? –
but he'd scarcely take time to be puzzled by poses
Criminals come in all sorts
as anyone knows who makes crosses
are as mad or sane as those who decide on their killings
Our one at least has been quiet so far
though they say he talked himself into this trouble
a carpenter's son who got notions of preaching

Well here's a carpenter's son who'll have carpenter sons
God willing   and build what's wanted
temples or tables   mangers or crosses
and shape them decently
working alone in that firm and profound abstraction
which blots out the bawling of rag-snatchers
To construct with hands   knee-weight   braced thigh
keeps the back turned from death

But it's too late now for the other carpenter's boy
to return to this peace before the nails are hammered

*Point Grey 1960*

## IRAPUATO

For reasons any
    brigadier
       could tell
this is a favourite
    nook
      for massacre
Toltex by Mixtex Mixtex by Aztex
Aztex by Spanishtex Spanishtex by Mexitex
by Mexitex by Mexitex by Texaco by Pemex

So any farmer can see how the strawberries
are the biggest
    and reddest
      in the whole damn continent
but why
   when arranged
     under the market flies
do they look like small clotting hearts?

*1955*

# THE BEAR ON THE DELHI ROAD

Unreal    tall as a myth
by the road the Himalayan bear
is beating the brilliant air
with his crooked arms
About him two men    bare
spindly as locusts    leap

One pulls on a ring
in the great soft nose    His mate
flicks    flicks with a stick
up at the rolling eyes

They have not led him here
down from the fabulous hills
to this bald alien plain
and the clamorous world    to kill
but simply to teach him to dance

They are peaceful both    these spare
men of Kashmir    and the bear
alive is their living    too
If    far on the Delhi way
around him galvanic they dance
it is merely to wear    wear
from his shaggy body the tranced
wish forever to stay
only an ambling bear
four-footed in berries

It is no more joyous for them
in this hot dust to prance
out of reach of the praying claws
sharpened to paw for ants
in the shadows of deodars
It is not easy to free
myth from reality
or rear this fellow up
to lurch    lurch with them
in the tranced dancing of men

*Srinagar 1958/Ile des Porquerolles 1959*

# CARIBBEAN KINGDOMS

Flowers live here as easily as air
They hang from power lines    they grow on light
A scalloped leaflet lying on a stair
will puff pink buds    and root itself in stone –
The animal hunts by day or pads within the night

The waxy jasmine    Indian arum    red mimosa
tangle unbruised    thigh to alien thigh
the dark Ashanti Blood    the yellow roses
keep peace beneath a prism sun –
White men alone the rainbow world deny

Stubborn as coral the crimson flowers rise
The torch plant towers higher than a man
Each dawn hibiscus gaze with newmade eyes
and cereus nightly stars the jungle roof –
The other kingdom rules what roosts it can

Petal and bract outdo the stir of sky
Their silent cockatoos in every park
preen and are fed without the need to fly
Coldly they nourish birds of heat    and shelter
all bony forms that cry before the dark

Still souls of butterflies the orchids poise
about the flaming trees and are not singed
Lilies turn spiders into spirit    dragons to toys
The Passion Flower lifts its crucifix unmanned –
Only the worlds of blood on suffering are hinged

When all the life of sound has milled
to silence I think these vines will find
a way to trumpet green and purple still
and jacarandas ring their bells down ruined streets –
Our kingdom comes and goes with mind

*Mona, Jamaica 1962*

## FOR GEORGE LAMMING

To you
    I can risk words about this

Mastering them   you know
    they are dull
        servants
who say less
    and worse
        than we feel

That party above Kingston Town
    we stood   five (six?) couples

linked singing
    more than rum happy

I was giddy
    from sudden friendship
wanted   undeserved

    black tulip faces

self swaying forgotten

    laughter in dance

Suddenly on a wall mirror
    my face assaulted me
stunned to see itself
    like a white snail
        in the supple dark flowers

Always now I move grateful
    to all of you
who let me walk thoughtless
    and unchallenged
in the gardens
    in the castles
        of your skins

*Off Haiti 1962*


## HOKKAI IN THE DEW LINE SNOWS


to sleep under real
stars    wake in the pupil of
original Sun

goodmornings with birds
love naked by waterfalls
o best planet –    whoooM!

a north door opens
the leaves scurry to hole &
the Cat prowls our world

*Trumansburg, N.Y. 1966*

**SHE IS**
*(for wai-lan, on her 24th birthday)*


she is
a little spruce tree
fresh every way
herself
like a dawn

when warm winds come
she will move
all her body
in a tremble of light

but today she stands
in magical stillness
she has clasped
all my falling flakes
from the round of her sky
and wished them
into her own
snowtree

through the cold time
she holds me
with evergreen
devotion
she bears up my whiteness

o so light may i press
letting each needle
grow in her own
symmetry

for i am at peace
in her form
after whirling
and faithful to all
her curves

but when warm winds come
we must stir from this trance
she will lift living arms
to the sun's dance

i will slide then
in a soft caress
of her brown sides
and my falling will end
somewhere in her roots

may my waters then
bring her strength only
help her hold trim
and evergreen her being
with suns and winds
for o many and many
and happiest years

*Treehouse, Uxbridge 1974*

# GEORGE BOWERING

## FAMILY

Was there power where I sprang from?
I wonder
            over the pondering of my past,
it must have begun with
                        hairpants prowlers of an earlier
Angle Land.   Picts, Jutes, Scots, carrying my seeds over a foggy
Island.   Families of Og, joining me to the Dukes of
Happy Land.

            Rich man
            poor man
            beggar man

            thief

In the descent & climbing, a tangled rime of time.

I know there was a singer of hymns in the centuries
& a peerage visited upon us.
                        & kings related & stories
told by idiots in stone houses.
                        Under thatcht roofs, others –
Sibilant growing of the Church & Nation
                        & the Clan.

To where we are, now.
                  No power but the delta of time.
No past unfogged on the Island.
                        No family but me.

# THE CRUMBLING WALL

A crumbling wall
is a good thing,

it saves a city,
this kind of city,

pushing itself north
wall against new wall.

The foundation
is crumbling, that

is the only way
a community can build.

Let the bricks
fall out. A broken

wall is a thing of
beauty, for a certain

time. Joy does not
last forever. It

requires change, it
must crumble to remain.

## I SAID I SAID

I said I said.

At the first glance you see there a singleness of intention,
to make the overly familiar
less exotic
to wash
it
away.

I was kicking the sea furiously,
bringing down fat smelly birds with a glance,
glamorizing my supper &
forcing it down too, it

all went down them days, even
with my friends who suspected
a frail bird of a large sort
inside that flesh, wings wet,
sagging. With bright bright eyes.

So I even managed to tell myself I wasnt faking when I sat at the table
late at night in Oliver & told my mother I'd rob her or anyone else to do
my writing. She thought of it as a hobby, an evening thing for a teacher,
an illusory aberration at least at first. Later a source of some balm among
the irritation.

A glance, one glance
at the real world would have saved so much time

but it was happily spent despite the railing
(the stage again)
against its ravages, that indulgence when yr young

I'll learn to do without birds
except where I fail at photographing them
or eat bits of them on occasion.

That is the gentle meal, not
talking too much yrself, waiting to hear
he said.

About I.


## POEM WRITTEN FOR GEORGE (1)


Poetry with politics in it
is small men answering back to volcanoes.

Volcanoes are upside down grails
knights look for
walking on their hands.

I never met a poet yet
who was a knight.

Knights are ignorant men with strong arms.

I never met a soldier yet
who was a poet.

Poets dont look for grails.

They want to drink from
the cups at hand.

Sometimes they climb mountains
to look down the middle
where mangled kings lie in a heap.

## THAT WAY, IN WORDS

I once thought I was Christ
come back, so later became a man who writes
because I came on him that way,
in words. To save the world or what
I knew of it, wanting to give & find
all goodness, still, but quick, of thought.

& now I am a male chauvinist to them,
to them a bourgeois liberal & to them an inter-
nationalist viper in our midst. Aw, our midst, I'd
just come back there after all that picturesque
James Dean cornermouth lonely dark walk street
high prairie existentialism. Now I juggle my evils
& try to look in faces one by one, some look back,
some dont.

## FIRST NIGHT OF FALL,
## GROSVENOR AVE

In the blue lamplight
the leaf falls

on its shadow

# LEONARD COHEN

## LOVERS

During the first pogrom they
Met behind the ruins of their homes –
Sweet merchants trading: her love
For a history-full of poems.

And at the hot ovens they
Cunningly managed a brief
Kiss before the soldier came
To knock out her golden teeth.

And in the furnace itself
As the flames flamed higher,
He tried to kiss her burning breasts
As she burned in the fire.

Later he often wondered:
Was their barter completed?
While men around him plundered
And knew he had been cheated.

## LETTER

How you murdered your family
means nothing to me
as your mouth moves across my body

And I know your dreams
of crumbling cities and galloping horses
of the sun coming too close
and the night never ending

but these mean nothing to me
beside your body

I know that outside a war is raging
that you issue orders
that babies are smothered and generals beheaded

but blood means nothing to me
it does not disturb your flesh

tasting blood on your tongue
does not shock me
as my arms grow into your hair

Do not think I do not understand
what happens
after the troops have been massacred
and the harlots put to the sword

And I write this only to rob you

that when one morning my head
hangs dripping with the other generals
from your house gate

that all this was anticipated
and so you will know that it meant nothing to me.

## YOU ALL IN WHITE

Whatever cities are brought down,
I will always bring you poems,
and the fruit of orchards
I pass by.

Strangers in your bed,
excluded by our grief,
listening to sleep-whispering,
will hear their passion beautifully explained,
and weep because they cannot kiss
your distant face.

Lovers of my beloved,
watch how my words put on her lips like clothes,
how they wear her body like a rare shawl.
Fruit is pyramided on the window-sill,
songs flutter against the disappearing wall.

The sky of the city
is washed in the fire
of Lebanese cedar and gold.
In smoky filigree cages
the apes and peacocks fret.
Now the cages do not hold,
in the burning street man and animal
perish in each other's arms,
peacocks drown around the melting throne.

Is it the king
who lies beside you listening?
Is it Solomon or David
or stuttering Charlemagne?
Is that his crown
in the suitcase beside your bed?

When we meet again,
you all in white,
I smelling of orchards,
when we meet –

But now you awaken,
and you are tired of this dream.
Turn toward the sad-eyed man.
He stayed by you all the night.
You will have something
to say to him.

## YOU HAVE THE LOVERS

You have the lovers,
they are nameless, their histories only for each other,
and you have the room, the bed and the windows.
Pretend it is a ritual.
Unfurl the bed, bury the lovers, blacken the windows,
let them live in that house for a generation or two.
No one dares disturb them.
Visitors in the corridor tip-toe past the long closed door,
they listen for sounds, for a moan, for a song:
nothing is heard, not even breathing.
You know they are not dead,
you can feel the presence of their intense love.
Your children grow up, they leave you,
they have become soldiers and riders.

Your mate dies after a life of service.
Who knows you? Who remembers you?
But in your house a ritual is in progress:
it is not finished: it needs more people.
One day the door is opened to the lovers' chamber.
The room has become a dense garden,
full of colours, smells, sounds you have never known.
The bed is smooth as a wafer of sunlight,
in the midst of the garden it stands alone.
In the bed the lovers, slowly and deliberately and silently,
perform the act of love.
Their eyes are closed,
as tightly as if heavy coins of flesh lay on them.
Their lips are bruised with new and old bruises.
Her hair and his beard are hopelessly tangled.
When he puts his mouth against her shoulder
she is uncertain whether her shoulder
has given or received the kiss.
All her flesh is like a mouth.
He carries his fingers along her waist
and feels his own waist caressed.
She holds him closer and his own arms tighten around her.
She kisses the hand beside her mouth.
It is his hand or her hand, it hardly matters,
there are so many more kisses.
You stand beside the bed, weeping with happiness,
you carefully peel away the sheets
from the slow-moving bodies.
Your eyes are filled with tears, you barely make out the lovers.
As you undress you sing out, and your voice is magnificent
because now you believe it is the first human voice
heard in that room.
The garments you let fall grow into vines.
You climb into bed and recover the flesh.
You close your eyes and allow them to be sewn shut.
You create an embrace and fall into it.
There is only one moment of pain or doubt
as you wonder how many multitudes are lying beside your body,
but a mouth kisses and a hand soothes the moment away.

## WHAT I'M DOING HERE

I do not know if the world has lied
I have lied
I do not know if the world has conspired against love
I have conspired against love
The atmosphere of torture is no comfort
I have tortured
Even without the mushroom cloud
still I would have hated
Listen
I would have done the same things
even if there were no death
I will not be held like a drunkard
under the cold tap of facts
I refuse the universal alibi

Like an empty telephone booth passed at night
and remembered
like mirrors in a movie palace lobby consulted
only on the way out
like a nymphomaniac who binds a thousand
into strange brotherhood
I wait
for each one of you to confess

**FOR   E. J. P.**


I once believed a single line
   in a Chinese poem could change
     forever how blossoms fell
and that the moon itself climbed on
   the grief of concise weeping men
     to journey over cups of wine
I thought invasions were begun for crows
   to pick at a skeleton
     dynasties sown and spent
to serve the language of a fine lament
   I thought governors ended their lives
     as sweetly drunken monks
telling time by rain and candles
   instructed by an insect's pilgrimage
     across the page – all this
so one might send an exile's perfect letter
to an ancient home-town friend

I chose a lonely country
   broke from love
     scorned the fraternity of war
I polished my tongue against the pumice moon
   floated my soul in cherry wine
     a perfumed barge for Lords of Memory
to languish on to drink to whisper out
   their store of strength
     as if beyond the mist along the shore
their girls their power still obeyed
   like clocks wound for a thousand years
I waited until my tongue was sore

Brown petals wind like fire around my poems
   I aimed them at the stars but
      like rainbows they were bent
before they sawed the world in half
   Who can trace the canyoned paths
      cattle have carved out of time
wandering from meadowlands to feasts
   Layer after layer of autumn leaves
      are swept away
Something forgets us perfectly


## ONE OF THE NIGHTS I
## DIDN'T KILL MYSELF


You dance on the day you saved
my theoretical angels
daughters of the new middle-class
who wear your mouths like Bardot
   Come my darlings
the movies are true
I am the lost sweet singer whose death
in the fog your new high-heeled boots
have ground into cigarette butts
I was walking the harbour this evening
looking for a 25-cent bed of water
but I will sleep tonight
with your garters curled in my shoes
like rainbows on vacation
with your virginity ruling
the condom cemeteries like a 2nd chance
I believe I believe
Thursday December 12th
is not the night
and I will kiss again the slope of a breast
little nipple above me
like a sunset

## YOU KNOW WHERE I HAVE BEEN

You know where I have been
Why my knees are raw
I'd like to speak to you
Who will see what I saw

Some men who saw me fall
Spread the news of failure
I want to speak to them
The dogs of literature

Pass me as I proudly
Passed the others
Who kneel in secret flight
Pass us proudly Brothers


## CLAIM ME, BLOOD, IF YOU
## HAVE A STORY

Claim me, blood, if you have a story
to tell with my Jewish face,
you are strong and holy still, only
speak, like the Zohar, of a carved-out place
into which I must pour myself like wine,
an emptiness of history which I must seize
and occupy, calm and full in this confine,
becoming clear "like good wine on its lees."

*1965*

## THE REASON I WRITE

The reason I write
is to make something
as beautiful as you are

When I'm with you
I want to be the kind of hero
I wanted to be
when I was seven years old
a perfect man
who kills

## A PERSON WHO EATS MEAT

A person who eats meat
wants to get his teeth into something
A person who does not eat meat
wants to get his teeth into something else
If these thoughts interest you for even a moment
you are lost

## THERE ARE NO TRAITORS AMONG WOMEN

There are no traitors among women
Even the mother does not tell the son
they do not wish us well

She cannot be tamed by conversation
Absence is the only weapon
against the supreme arsenal of her body

She reserves a special contempt
for the slaves of beauty
She lets them watch her die

Forgive me, partisans,
I only sing this for the ones
who do not care who wins the war

# THIS IS THE POEM WE HAVE BEEN WAITING FOR

This is the poem we have been waiting for
n'est-ce pas
Much returns to us when we read it
which we do over and over again
It is not inspired
It took days and days to write
You are a detail in it
then you are the engine of the song
If only your gorilla was dead
we could be lovers
You cannot accuse my poem of helping anyone
You cannot use the tone
for the construction of a new thing
We like to read it slowly
touching ourselves
while falling asleep in the charcoal tower
after the terrible goodbye
We stop here and there
to put up red curtains or change the cats
but we come back
filled with sweet gratitude
O sweet gratitude
to be the ones we are
drivers of cars in the night-time rain
toward the adult restaurants and the toughest of lives
in Nashville and Acapulco

# LOUIS DUDEK

## SELECTIONS FROM *EUROPE*


**1**

Cleaving out through the clean St. Lawrence,
cellophane sweeps crisp with contemporaneity,
the shores receding . . .
                              going out to sea. . . .

                                        Bridge
parties in the lounge,
              and tourist chatter:

Time's newest, flimsiest, cheapest crinkles
              unwrapping Vacation Tours –
"Let's finish this hand"
              "I've had enough"

Travelling tourist class, to Europe
              out of American, Canadian cities.
What are we going to find?
              What are we going to see?

**10**

But I had not known the sea would be this splendid
                              magnificent lady:
"destroyer of ships, of cities"
in luxurious ermine and leopard coat
                              sighing in the ship's wake;

destroyer of civilizations, of pantheons,
to whom Greece and Rome are only a row of white breakers
spilled with a hush, in air,
then marbled patterns on a smoother wave. . . .

And I would not be surprised if the sea made Time
in which to build and to destroy
as it builds these waves and indolently breaks them,
                    or if the whole fiction
of living were only a coil in her curvature
                    of immense imagination.

Maker and breaker of nations, sea of resources,
you have enough here for a million rivers,
                    for a billion cities,
enough for new Judea, for new Alexandria,
and Paris once again, and America's morning.

## 19

The commotion of these waves, however strong, cannot disturb
                    the compass-line of the horizon
nor the plumb-line of gravity, because this cross coordinates
                    the tragic pulls of necessity
that chart the ideal endings, for waves, and storms
                    and sunset winds:
the dead scattered on the stage in the fifth act
– Cordelia in Lear's arms, Ophelia, Juliet, all silent –
show nature restored to order and just measure.
                    The horizon is perfect,
and nothing can be stricter
than gravity; in relation to these
                    the stage is rocked and tossed,
kings fall with their crowns, poets sink with their laurels.

**26**

It's a small world, a very small world
                we move in,
but it takes us by the heart,
                      takes us in
before we know it, and we hate to part with it.

The gesture was really significant,
                on new land, we thought it important
and we took pictures, of each putting his first foot on it.

Meeting and parting, the champagne
                of life goes to these occasions.

We have left our world, we have left America,
                and we are here.


## THE SEA AT MONHEGAN


Torrent and torment, the ocean's revel
of spawning and eating
the spit of one another, rocky toothsome scarabs,
stinking sea-kelp, barnacles and scales –

out of which the white reef,
sea-gull, tuna,

the eye, and the delicate reaching heart's
                anemone.

Its designation, like wing marks or fins
or the manyshapes of the marine flora:
a mind – to hurt, or amuse
with skies, seascapes, truths!

Then lost in that great indifference
(as it is a great concern)
our fitful lives on this volcanic island,

a living green in mid-ocean,
a lick of the too-great energy,

that these hills in their sequences, swells,
wrap and fold, nurse to their mother rhythms.


## AT LAC EN COEUR


### 1

What kind of honey does a bee get from a thistle?
A purple bomb, toxic
            with spears of language.

Hating pretentiousness,
            or the vanity of writing poems,
I sit for hours without a word.

The hidden bios, cosmos, works with his emotions
shaping things into multiform shapes of desire.

He never says a word
            nor even (perhaps) thinks a thought
but fits the liver under the beating heart
as the artist places his cove and tree,
            feeling his way
            to the complex unities.

We cross-section this work of love
            when we think or talk.

**2**

Nothing is eternal. Not even the trees
though I gather that some are longer-lived than a man.

A whirling flashlight
          makes a permanent wheel.
Moving lights. We are a web.

Unity, out of motion and diversity,
          as real as atoms.

The blue sky turning pale green at the horizon,
only one streak of cloud
          beyond the birch leaves overhead.

The trees, cedar, some maple, and tattered pine,
below them the fern and smaller brush,

dead leaves, brown earth, rock
(a canoe on the still water makes a slapping sound)

And I sit, the ache in my bones receding,
          a thought breathing cold air –

shaping a world already made
          to a form that I require.

# JOHN GLASSCO

## THE ENTAILED FARM

A footpath would have been enough.
The muddy mile of side-road has no purpose
Save as it serves for others to link up
Crossroads marked on the map with a nameless cross
By way of these choked and heartless fields of paintbrush
And the mute, sealed house,

Where the spring's tooth, stripping shingles, scaling
Beam and clapboard, probes for the rot below
Porch and pediment and blind bow-window,
And the wooden trunk with the coloured cardboard lining
Lies where it fell when the wall of the flying wing
Fell down ten years ago;

Where the stone wall is a haven for snake and squirrel,
The steepled dovecote for phoebe and willow-wren,
And the falling field-gates, trigged by an earthen swell,
Open on a wild where nothing is raised or penned,
On rusty acres of witch-grass and wild sorrel
Where the field-birds cry and contend.

You, tourist, salesman, family out for a picnic,
Who saw the bearded man that walked like a bear,
His pair of water-pails slung from a wooden neckyoke,
Slipping in by the woodshed – Come away,
That naked door is proof against all knocking!
Standing and knocking there,

You might as well expect time's gate to open
On the living past, the garden bloom again,
The house stand upright, hay-barn's swayback coping
Stiffen, and see as in a fretted frame
Men in the meadow and a small boy whooping
The red oxen down that orchard lane,

Or revive the slow strong greed of the coffined farmer
Who cleared, stumped, fenced, rotating sinew and sweat,
Beating the ploughshare into an honest dollar,
Who living and dying planned to cheat time's night
Through the same white-bearded boy – who is hiding somewhere
Now, till you're out of sight,

And have left him alone: alone with the grief or anger
Or whatever it is that flickers but will not die
In the dull brain of the victim turned avenger,
At war with a shadow, in flight from passers-by,
From us – who are free from all but the hint of attainder,
Who can meet a stranger's eye

With a good face, can answer a question, give a reason,
For whom the world's fields and fences stand up plain,
Nor dazzle in sunlight or crumble behind the rain:
From us, with our hearts but lightly tinged with poison,
Who composed our quarrel early and in good season
Buried the hatchet in our father's brain.

# THE CARDINAL'S DOG
*(Musée d'Autun)*


The unknown Master of Moulins
Painted the Nativity: we see
The stable, the stupid ox and Mary,
Simpering Joseph on his knees
And the Cardinal Rolin on his knees too,
His red robe centred by a rat-faced dog.

They all look at each other: Joseph at Mary,
Mary (her face is blue) at the child,
The Cardinal looks, if anywhere, at the ox;
But the child looks at the little dog,
And the dog at nothing, simply being well-behaved:
He is the one who feels and knows. . . .

Pensive little dog (you that I love
Being only flesh and blood) you see
The reason for all this, the dying need
Of the worshipful, the master: so
We are all one, have seen the birth of God

Either through eyes of friend or master,
In a book, a song, a landscape or a child,
For a breath of time are immortal, tuned
To the chord and certainties of animal hope.
And the picture *teaches us* – as Balzac would say –
To trust anything on earth more than man.

## THOMAS À KEMPIS

His unsubsistent mind, self-moving and
Subject to *rerum horror*, could observe
– Before its descent into the nightly grave –
Not that the cell expands, but the prisoner
Diminishes himself, not that he's brave,
But that, on earth, there's nothing left to fear.
Nobodaddy held him in his hand,

A fireless particle. I think we are
Coals ever cooling, blown at times by God;
And whether to strike or suffer for the good
Of all that breath has meant divides my hours,
And though to strike, to inch the door abroad,
Is all my vision allows (that – merciful powers! –
Confounds the firefly and the falling star),

The stroke or sufferance in the midnight is
An orchestral sigh. Always the cell is here,
Stronger than fire, than the release of fear,
Than any love that I can answer for. . . .
But oh, green leaves and singing birds that see
The flaming sun, lie, lie of the open door,
The air of that bright heaven that is not his!

## BRUMMELL AT CALAIS

A foolish useless man who had done nothing
All his life long but keep himself clean,
Locked in the glittering armour of a pose
Made up of impudence, chastity and reserve –
How does his memory still survive his world?

The portraits show us only a tilted nose,
Lips full blown, a cravat and curly wig,
And a pair of posturing eyes,
Infinitely vulnerable, deeply innocent,
Their malice harmless as a child's:

And he has returned to childhood now, his stature
That of the Butterfly whose *Funeral*
He sang (his only song) for one of his
Dear duchesses, Frances or Georgiana,
In the intolerable metre of Tom Moore –

To a childhood of sweet biscuits and curaçao;
Hair-oil and tweezers make him forget his debts,
The angle of his hat remains the same,
His little boots pick their way over the cobblestones,
But where is he going as well as going mad?

Nowhere: his glory is already upon him,
The fading Regency man who will leave behind
More than the ankle-buttoning pantaloon!
For see, even now in the long implacable twilight,
The triumph of his veritable art,

An art of being, nothing but being, the grace
Of perfect self-assertion based on nothing,
As in our vanity's cause against the void
He strikes his elegant blow, the solemn report of those
Who have done nothing and will never die.

## ONE LAST WORD
*For M. McC.*


Now that I have your hand, let me persuade you
The means are more important than the end,
Ends being only an excuse for action,
For adventures sought for their own sake alone,
Pictures along the way, feelings
Released in love: so, acting out our dreams
We justify movement by giving it a purpose
(Who can be still forever?)
This is the rationale of travel
And the formula of lovers.

Dearest, it is not for the amusement of certain tissues,
Nor for whatever may thread our loins like a vein
                                    of miraculous water
That now (under the music) I speak your name –
But for the journey we shall take together
Through a transfigured landscape
Of beasts and birds and people
Where everything is new.
                        Listen,
The embarkation for Cythera
Is eternal because it ends nowhere:
No port for those tasselled sails! And for our love
No outcome,
Only the modesty
The perfection
Of the flight or death of a bird.

# PHYLLIS GOTLIEB

## HOSPITALITY

Da Vinci and the man on the bed stare
at each other through the dark air of
death watch. The dying man more than half
suspects from the black glitter
beneath the eaved brows that it is Death
watching;

        Da Vinci moodily
hones in his mind the silver
saw he has made to trepan the skull.

## HAIKU ON BRUEGHEL

burning on the snow
drag-footed across the fields
whiskey-faced men go

the blind lead the blind
and coarse oglers invade the
countries of the mind

Icarus falling
makes what mark on the seas where
wild birds are calling

can children who play
a thousand multicoloured
games be dead today?

# PARADIGM

Through the summer windows of afternoon
sunslanted, an old woman
stout and ungainly who lugs
jars of pickled herring to the least
grateful of daughters-in-law
calls suddenly
*Jane!*
in a young girl's voice to the youngest
*I see you, Jane!*
tottering granddaughter, piercing other
echoes of the girl
running the dusty streets of a Polish village
*I catch you!*
fifty years ago.

Sometimes on a country porch
a gap-toothed crone in a checkered kerchief holding
a toothless child high between twisted hands
utters a nameless necessary battle-cry.

I see my children have all my proud faults
no changelings: endless
red ribbons braided
into the child's blood go skimming
unfathomable steps of light.

# MATINÉE

The monkey stops his
to-and-fro to the chain's end only
to toss off a trick
with a back flip arrogant
as a Spanish grandee, in body
slender and muscular, a
tempered coil on the chance
a link may snap
                          cocking
the narrow cynic eye

his honed critical face set against
the pushback bowler and pocky nose of his man, he
signals
with the sprung whorl of his tail: I'm on
a chain, but by God I keep it taut.

## SUB ROSA

I don't know why, but robins choose
our crazy trellis-fence for the house
beautiful; stick straw string mud anything
goes, motherbird
deeps it with her bronze
burnisher; the secret hours out
4 copper sulphate globes kids
palm in sweaty hatchery while she
heads for the wormfront; one falls,
one vanishes, 2 wet nurslings break
shell, kids bear away empty
prizes, catspaw the begonias, fledglings
barbaric yawp earth & sky, kids
lift them, leave enriched
breadcrumbs in the murphy bed, motherbird
climbs the sunbeam, careless
as a mechanical
nightingale but
somehow
one
puffed
broody speckled
as an egg and ovoid youngster
survives kids going kitchycoo
and his cold bed, sums up the lot
                                    become
thrice bigger than his dam, hangs around the
kitchen in his striped sweater, gulping
a slug now & then, a lubberly
caliban; well, she's
no momist, heaves the lout
over the side, he shrieks! scrunches in nakedeye
beam of the sun snivelling
for a soft featherwing of his ma, hops
here & there, weeps, noplacetogo, we chase
the fluffy lummox all round our yard

and the neighbours' scared of dogs, find
him a fencepost
                    trembles
grieves you'll-be-sorry, makes excuses, wets
his foot in the air and gets off
the pad at last;
                    merrywidow having flown the
coop lies open to the wandering
cuckoo


## FIRST PERSON DEMONSTRATIVE


I'd rather
heave half a brick than say
I love you, though I do
I'd rather
crawl in a hole than call you
darling, though you are
I'd rather
wrench off an arm than hug you though
it's what I long to do
I'd rather
gather a posy of poison ivy than
ask if you love me

so if my
hair doesn't stand on end it's because
I never tease it
and if my
heart isn't in my mouth it's because
it knows its place
and if I
don't take a bite of your ear it's because
gristle gripes my guts
and if you
miss the message better get new
glasses and read it twice

# RALPH GUSTAFSON

## PROLOGUE TO SUMMER

Quick at the maple's root
The woodchuck garbles leaves,
Flung from its tooth
Flake of sun.

Under the gangrened stump
Slugs drag slime,
The fieldmouse gnaws
The crust of air.

Smell! – the leaf-mould smokes,
At the water-edge flapped
By the waves a fish
Belly-up stinking.

Soil thaws. The ice
Rotted from broken wharf
Where last-year's coin
Is silver gotten.

Male-naked the air. Compel!
Urgent the deed, urgent
And muscular the dream
Invaginate!

## FLIGHT INTO DARKNESS

We have fulfilled our apprehension, hope,
Matched our hands' delay against the sun,
Against a guttering candle written dreams.
Was it today we fumbled spiral of spring,
Clutched at the throat the knot of accurate winds,
Noose and thong by beauty slung?

Yesterday yesterday! the hills were bare of snow,
The hackneyed maple broke with leaf, the bough
Sprang colour along the sweetened air – whose action
Pledged our anger. O we have sworn our lives
Between the hyphened prologue of the crow,
The crimson coming of the rose!

Who now, regretting June with adult smiles,
Set nodding with a finger Buddha's porcelain head:
Hearing of marvels in the township, turned
Expensive keys against the empty street,
From possible cars saw moon eclipse the sun,
Cautious glass before our eyes.

And all that year the tamarack was green
And we who saw the tolerant seed and snow,
By leaning questions ambushed. Grace was then
The grateful turning-out of lamps at night,
Within the book the treacherous flower's clue,
The short escape of perjured love.

For we remembering our defense refused
The mirror's prosecution, praised the speaker
On the chairman's right: within the files,
Found brief anger for the anonymous clock,
Looking up, the calendar on startled walls –
Withdrawing truth from blundering sleep.

We have waited important letters from the west,
In evening cities heard the newspaper tossed
Against the door, under the prosperous valley
Guessed at oil, proved the legend false.
We dream wisely who once had loved too well.
And yet, coming on sun across

An alien street, stand suddenly surprised –
As Galileo, before his midnight window,
Cloak about his shoulders, coldly chose
A fatal planet – first, listened while
The solitary wagon passed along the road –
Then aimed his contradictory lens.


## IN THE YUKON


In Europe, you can't move without going down into history.
Here, all is a beginning. I saw a salmon jump,
Again and again, against the current,
The timbered hills a background, wooded green
Unpushed through; the salmon jumped, silver.
This was news, was commerce, at the end of the summer
The leap for dying. Moose came down to the water edge
To drink and the salmon turned silver arcs.
At night, the northern lights played, great over country
Without tapestry and coronations, kings crowned
With weights of gold. They were green,
Green hangings and great grandeur, over the north
Going to what no man can hold hard in mind,
The dredge of that gravity, being without experience.

## AT THE OCEAN'S VERGE

I should pray but my soul is stopt.
This is a bombast world: fig-trees,
Snow, macacos, ocean's hurl
And surf and surge, on applebough
As crag whose cave holds kraken or
With comb of coral mermaid cuddles.
All's mad majesty and squander,
And x and y or zodiac
Excreting wizard mathematics
Like a slew of ebbtide worms
Won't solve it. The sand is miles and packt
And moonlights wash the gnawings of
A million years. The globe cants so,
It's miracle a man can walk it.
Listen to him: *I'll say my prayers*
*And set mine eyes on kingdom come.*
*I'll jump the prickly hedge and scratch*
*Them in again.* I'll. I'll.
Not Hesperides, I warrant,
No matter what you will. Try.
Scour this heaven-hung kettle of fish –
The sweep has greater satisfaction
Up a chimney cleaning soot
With good soap after. Oh, you'll hoist
And heft your stature by a hair –
No one but the Barber wiser.
     Hear how this ocean thurls and thunders!
     Crashing foams and ravels once
     Was muted marble Athens owned.

# NOW AT THE OCEAN'S VERGE

After great expectations, what
It is the time of life declares, that
Was there, is as the ebbtide shows:
These miles of sand packt and under a slant
Moon, the piling granite throw of surf,
Nothing but the beauty of itself.
Conch and shell and tugged weed cling
To the wave and are thrown.
      I turn to the seamark,
Climb descensions of pebbles and under the moon
Sit arms on knees, the night of stars,
Each in apportioned stance, intolerable before
The initialling mind. Indigence is all.
Concrete heaven only must suffice,
What expectation thought was possible:
Reduced sand; a grasp, whorled and beautiful,
Tossed by the tide, this accessible,
Reached for, empty shell.

## MEANWHILE, THESE PERFECT DETAILS

The ragged sublime mocks us.
How easy upon the sense
This flower steals, taken
From the sill of terror, arduously
Got against the mountain's
Unfinished icy glory –
Perfection; as though a grace,
All its meaning in
Repose.

       Not this
Sublimity, this glacier crushed
On the sides of our descent,
These locked cliffs, unfinished,
Towering the soul until
Meeting a whirling wind,
There's short achievement, breath
In the lungs a lapse, a mockery,
Though we meanwhile stand
On this scarp of flowers, below us
Height, height above,
In perfect resolution;
The ironic majesty,
As of the overhead stars,
From it, a flower taken.


## KAKUYU PRINT

The man walks past the
Flower. Frogs slap their sides, the
Hare rolls with laughter.

# DAVID HELWIG

## LATE OCTOBER

The park,
when the gates are closed,
gives itself to the wind.

Leaves drift and fall
to the wet earth.
The electric train,
the merry-go-round
are gone.

Crows move
under the clouds.

The iron gates are closed.

Among the leaves
lies a broken gaudy horse
from the merry-go-round,
legs snapped off,
body brought to earth,
a wooden Pegasus,
stiff with gaiety and colour,
the magic circle of his path
broken.

And the empty park
spins like a merry-go-round

around his wooden eye.

## RETURN

After the white nights
of solitaire
within the prison of the winter heart,
only the dead
can speak of less than daffodils
or singing birds,
bright feathered birds.

But the first to return
are crows,
black scavengers
strutting awkwardly over the spring earth.

Only black birds
that live close to death
can come here.

But strident as they are
we must love them
just for their speaking of rebirth.

# IMAGINARY EVENING, REAL DARK

The dark animals
look about
softly for darkness.

The warm furry
night-eyed
delvers and weavers
test the air
on the open slopes.

Small mice lift their soft
brownish nuzzling noses
and frightened, retire.

Night climbs down the web of sky
and lies among them.

# VISION

This is the night when the anarchist dreams of heaven
and gives his dreams away by handfuls.

The Bolsheviks burn. Their eyes have turned to guns.

This is the night when the anarchist dreams of love.

The Bolsheviks burn like paper.

This is the night when the anarchist dreams of freedom,
his dream so rich and deep
that after he wakes, sweating and shaking,
he doesn't dare remember it.
And this is the night when the anarchist dreams of peace,
a place of silence where no-one is ravaged
by the travelling teeth of the hours.

This is the night when the Bolsheviks burn.

Someone is here. Open your doors.

## DRUNKEN POEM

Afternoon is invading my eyes.
Between here and the barn
the fallen leaves lie untouched.
I never rake the lawn, I never
clean the car. The children
squabble all round me
as the day darkens and beer
darkens my brain and the thought
of you and a thousand confusions
darken my heart, and I find
a photograph on the table
of a newborn child. My child, I think,
my Kate who now stands near me,
grown, difficult, beloved, and I find
the threat of tears invading my eyes.

Oh sentimental absurd man, who
can you think you are, writing
this something, nothing, drunken words
that solve nothing and say
nothing, only that I know
nothing and that the earth
is the body of a god and you
and I are the body of a god.

The children laugh. I remember
the night that Kate was born.

All afternoon I have said to myself
that love is too simple, is only
an easy death. I think of the men
and women who are puzzled at me
and what they have heard me say.

I am the eyes of god, I am
the tongue of god and so are you
and you and you, even dying,
even hating the world to death.

Rhetoric, beer rhetoric, I have nothing
to claim but a willingness to lose.

I wear a child's Indian headdress.
I write with a ball-point pen.
My brain is addled by beer,
by the coming of dark, by the love
of death, by you, by all the times
that I didn't know what I was doing.

The trees are black against the blue air
as the paper boy does his rounds
and the day becomes gone. Time,
death, loving; we can only live
by being in love with loss, with disaster.

There is no conclusion to this poem. Ever.

*unfinished poem*
*of any aesthetics of*
*the incomplete.*

# GEORGE JOHNSTON

## LOVE OF THE CITY

After a week of wandering through the world
Eating wherever we could, sleeping, washing ourselves
Wherever we could, in bars and railway rooms,
We came to this great city. Nothing
Will persuade us ever to leave it again.

The city loves us now it's moved us in:
The yellow sky comes down and fills the room;
Dirt on the floor is kind, the walls are kind,
Everyone's kind to us wherever we go.

And truly when death comes where will he find
A better room than here, better arrangements,
More courtesy, more eager friendliness
Than in this excellent street-scattered city,
This home, this network, this great roof of pity?

# WAR ON THE PERIPHERY

Around the battlements go by
Soldier men against the sky,
Violent lovers, husbands, sons,
Guarding my peaceful life with guns.

My pleasures, how discreet they are!
A little booze, a little car,
Two little children and a wife
Living a small suburban life.

My little children eat my heart;
At seven o'clock we kiss and part,
At seven o'clock we meet again;
They eat my heart and grow to men.

I watch their tenderness with fear
While on the battlements I hear
The violent, obedient ones
Guarding my family with guns.

## MONEY IN POCKET

I've got money in my pockets,
Excellent pockets because there's money in them;
I can't feel low while there's paper for my fingers
In my excellent pockets, Caesar's mark on it.

I've got children in my rooms,
Blood-borne hostages, arrows from my side:
I can't sleep heavy while they're breathing in their beds
Who burst through my passageways and grow me back to earth.

I've got time in my clocks
And beer in my cellar and spiders in my windows:
I can't spend time nor drink all the beer
And I feel in the spread web the spider's small eye.


## SPRING MOON

Moon in a town sky,
Half shut, dark one way from the middle,
Above a creek with spring peepers.

Homeward all alone, after joy,
Hands in pockets, making a thoughtful way
Over the bridge, down the street.

No voices, no women,
Only peepers,
And a solemn unsteadiness of all things.

## US TOGETHER

I do not like anything the way I
like you in your underwear I like you
and in your party clothes o my in your
party clothes and with nothing on at all
you do not need to wear a thing at all
for me to like you and you may talk or
not talk I like you either way nothing
makes me feel so nearly at home on Earth
as just to be with you and say nothing.

## INDOORS

Says the window
    what heart
    in this weather?

Says the blizzard
    outdoors.

Says the pond
    slow blood
    deep down
    in hard mud.

Says the world
    no peace
    no shelter.

Says music
    the life.

Says the evening
  shut.

Says the stove
  hot iron
  hot breath
  in the pipes.

Good night.

## NONSTOP JETFLIGHT TO HALIFAX

Never such comfort, annihilation
of the way there. But that's me! I
am the way there. These blandishments, these
knees and elbows bringing me food and drink
in high sunshine over high cloud

  to distract me.

Now that we're so far up why don't we stay?

Non-question of a non-questioner
as the stewardess knows having
smiled on my effacement.
But she gives me a look.
Never mind, I say. Sit down
beside me. Perhaps on me.

# A. M. KLEIN

## SWEET SINGER

O what would David say,
Young David in the fields,
Singing in Bethlehem,
Were he to hear this day
Old Mendel slowly hum
His sweetest songs,
Old Mendel, who being poor,
Cannot through charity
Atone his wrongs,
And being ignorant,
Cannot in learned wise
Win Paradise,
Old Mendel who begs Heaven as his alms
By iterating and re-iterating psalms?

## JOB REVILES

God is grown ancient. He no longer hears.
He has been deafened by his perfect thunders.
With clouds for cotton he has stopped his ears.

The Lord is purblind; and his heaven sunders
Him from the peccadillos of this earth.
He meditates his youth; he dreams; he wonders.

His cherubs have acquired beards and girth.
They cannot move to do his bidding. Even
The angels yawn. Satan preserves his mirth.

How long, O Lord, will Israel's heart be riven?
How long will we cry to a dotard God
To let us keep the breath that He has given?

How long will you sit on your throne, and nod?


## SIMEON TAKES HINTS FROM HIS ENVIRONS

Heaven is God's grimace at us on high.
This land is a cathedral; speech, its sermon.
The moon is a rude gargoyle in the sky.

The leaves rustle. Come, who will now determine
Whether this be the wind, or priestly robes.
The frogs croak out ecclesiastic German,

Whereby our slavish ears have punctured lobes.
The stars are mass-lamps on a lofty altar;
Even the angels are Judaeophobes.

There is one path; in it I shall not falter.
Let me rush to the bosom of the state
And church, grasp lawyer-code and monkish psalter,

And being Christianus Simeon, late
Of Jewry, have much comfort and salvation –
Salvation in this life, at any rate.


## ONCE IN A YEAR


Once in a year this comes to pass:
My father is a king in a black skull cap,
My mother is a queen in a brown perruque,
A princess my sister, a lovely lass,
My brother a prince, and I a duke.

Silver and plate, and fine cut-glass
Brought from the cupboards that hid them till now
Banquet King David's true lineage here.
Once in a year this comes to pass,
Once in a long unroyal year.

## PSALM XXXVI: A PSALM TOUCHING GENEALOGY

Not sole was I born, but entire genesis:
For to the fathers that begat me, this
Body is residence. Corpuscular,
They dwell in my veins, they eavesdrop at my ear,
They circle, as with Torahs, round my skull,
In exit and in entrance all day pull
The latches of my heart, descend, and rise –
And there look generations through my eyes.


## AND IN THAT DROWNING INSTANT

And in that drowning instant as
the water heightened over me
it suddenly did come to pass
my preterite eternity
the image of myself intent
on several freedoms

                  fading to
myself in yellowed basel-print
vanishing

       into ghetto Jew
a face among the faces of
the rapt disciples hearkening
the raptures of the Baalshem Tov
explaining Torah

<pre>
            vanishing
amidst the water's flickering green
to show me in old Amsterdam
which topples

            into a new scene
Cordova where an Abraham
faces inquisitors

            the face
is suddenly beneath an arch
whose Latin script the waves erase
and flashes now the backward march
of many

        I among them

            to
Jerusalem-gate and Temple-door!
</pre>

*For the third time my body rises*
*And finds the good, the lasting shore!*

# MEDITATION UPON SURVIVAL

At times, sensing that the golgotha'd dead
run plasma through my veins, and that I must live
their unexpired six million circuits, giving
to each of their nightmares my body for a bed –
inspirited, dispirited –
those times that I feel their death-wish bubbling the
channels of my blood –
I grow bitter at my false felicity –
the spared one – and would almost add my wish
for the centigrade furnace and the cyanide flood.

However, one continues to live, though mortally.
O, like some frightened, tattered, hysterical man
run to a place of safety – the whole way run –
whose lips, now frenzy-foamed, now delirium-dry
cry out the tenses of the verb to die.
cry love, cry loss, being asked: *And yet unspilled
your own blood?* weeps, and makes
his stuttering innocence a kind of guilt –
O, like that man am I, bereaved and suspect,
convicted with the news my mourning breaks.

Us they have made the monster, made that thing
that lives though cut in three: the severed head
which breathes, looks on, hears, thinks, weeps, and is bled
continuously with a drop by drop longing
for its members' re-membering!
And, the torn torso, spilling heart and lights
and the cathartic dregs!
These, for the pit! Upon the roads, the flights –
– O how are you reduced, my people, cut down to a limb! –
upon the roads the flights of the bodiless legs.

Myself to recognize: a curio;
the atavism of some old coin's face;
one who, though watched and isolate, does go –
the last point of a diminished race –
the way of the fletched buffalo.
Gerundive of extinct. An original.
What else, therefore, to do
but leave these bones that are not ash to fill –
O not my father's vault – but the glass-case
some proud museum catalogues *Last Jew.*


## POLITICAL MEETING
*(For Camillien Houde)*


On the school platform, draping the folding seats,
they wait the chairman's praise and glass of water.
Upon the wall the agonized Y initials their faith.

Here all are laic; the skirted brothers have gone.
Still, their equivocal absence is felt, like a breeze
that gives curtains the sounds of surplices.

The hall is yellow with light, and jocular;
suddenly some one lets loose upon the air
the ritual bird which the crowd in snares of singing

catches and plucks, throat, wings, and little limbs.
Fall the feathers of sound, like *alouette's.*
The chairman, now, is charming, full of asides and wit,

building his orators, and chipping off
the heckling gargoyles popping in the hall.
(Outside, in the dark, the street is body-tall,

flowered with faces intent on the scarecrow thing
that shouts to thousands the echoing
of their own wishes.) The Orator has risen!

Worshipped and loved, their favourite visitor,
a country uncle with sunflower seeds in his pockets,
full of wonderful moods, tricks, imitative talk,

he is their idol: like themselves, not handsome,
not snobbish, not of the *Grande Allée! Un homme!*
Intimate, informal, he makes bear's compliments

to the ladies; is gallant; and grins;
goes for the balloon, his opposition, with pins;
jokes also on himself, speaks of himself

in the third person, slings slang, and winks with folklore;
and knows now that he has them, kith and kin.
Calmly, therefore, he begins to speak of war,

praises the virtue of being *Canadien,*
of being at peace, of faith, of family,
and suddenly his other voice: *Where are your sons?*

He is tearful, choking tears; but not he
would blame the clever English; in their place
he'd do the same; maybe.

Where *are* your sons?
                              The whole street wears one face,
shadowed and grim; and in the darkness rises
the body-odour of race.

## LOOKOUT: MOUNT ROYAL

Remembering boyhood, it is always here
the boy in blouse and kneepants on the road
trailing his stick over the hopscotched sun;
or here, upon the suddenly moving hill;
or at the turned tap its cold white mandarin mustaches;
or at the lookout, finally,
breathing easy, standing still

to click the eye on motion forever stopped:
the photographer's tripod and his sudden faces
buoyed up by water on his magnet caught
still smiling as if under water.still;
the exclamatory tourists descending the *calèches;*
the maids in starch; the ladies in white gloves;
other kids of other slums and races;
and on the bridle-paths
the horsemen on their horses like the tops of f 's:

or from the parapet make out
beneath the green marine
the discovered road, the hospital's romantic
gables and roofs, and all the civic Euclid
running through sunken parallels and lolling
in diamond and square, then proud-pedantical
with spire and dome
making its way to the sought point, his home.

home recognized: there: to be returned to –

lets the full birdseye circle to the river,
its singsong bridges, its mapmaker curves, its
island with the two shades of green, meadow and wood;
and circles round that water-tower'd coast;
then, to the remote rhapsodic mountains; then,
– and to be lost –
to clouds like white slow friendly animals
which all the afternoon across his eyes
will move their paced spaced footfalls.

# STANCE OF THE AMIDAH

*O Lord, open Thou my lips; and my mouth shall declare Thy praise:*

God of Abraham, God of Isaac, God of Jacob, who hast bound
to the patriarchs their posterity and hast made Thyself manifest
in the longings of men and hast condescended to bestow upon
history a shadow of the shadows of Thy radiance;
Who with the single word hast made the world, hanging before
us the heavens like an unrolled scroll, and the earth old manuscript,
and the murmurous sea, each, all-allusive to Thy glory, so that
from them we might conjecture and surmise and almost know Thee;

> *Whom only angels know*
> *Who in Thy burning courts*
> *Cry:* Holy! Holy! Holy!
> *While mortal voice below*
> *With seraphim consorts*
> *To murmur:* Holy! Holy!
> *Yet holiness not know.*

Favour us, O Lord, with understanding, who hast given to
the bee its knowledge and to the ant its foresight, to the sleeping
bear Joseph's prudence, and even to the dead lodestone its instinct
for the star, favour us with understanding of what in the
inscrutable design is for our doomsday-good;
Oh, give us such understanding as makes superfluous second
thought; and at Thy least, give us to understand to repent.
At the beginning of our days Thou dost give – oh, at the end,
forgive!
Deem our affliction worthy of Thy care, and now with a last
redeeming, Redeemer of Israel, redeem!
Over our fevers pass the wind of Thy hand; against our chills,
Thy warmth. O great Physician, heal us! and shall we ailing
be healed.

From want deliver us. Yield the earth fruitful. Let rain a
delicate stalk, let dew in the bright seed, sprout ever abundance.
Shelter us behind the four walls of Thy seasons, roof us with
justice, O Lord, who settest the sun to labour for our evening dish!

Thyself do utter the Shma! Sound the great horn of our
freedom, raise up the ensign of freedom, and gather from the four
corners of the earth, as we do gather the four fringes to kiss them,
Thy people, Thy folk, rejected Thine elect.

Restore our judges as in former times restore our Judge. Blessed
art Thou, O Lord, King, who loves righteousness and judgment.

Favour them, O Lord, Thy saints Thy paupers, who do forgo
all other Thy benedictions for the benediction of Thy name.

Oh, build Jerusalem!

Anoint Thy people David!

Our prayers accept, but judge us not through our prayers:
grant them with mercy.

Make us of Thy love a sanctuary, an altar where the heart may
cease from fear, and evil a burnt offering is consumed away, and
good, like the fine dust of spices, an adulation of incense, rises up.

Oh, accept, accept, accept our thanks for the day's three
miracles, of dusk, of dawn, of noon, and of the years which with
Thy presence are made felicitous.

Grant us – our last petition – peace, Thine especial blessing,
which is of Thy grace and of the shining and the turning of Thy
Face.

# IRVING LAYTON

## THE BLACK HUNTSMEN

Before ever I knew men were hunting me
I knew delight as water in a glass in a pool;
The childish heart then
Was ears nose eyes twiceten fingers,
And the torpid slum street, in summer,
A cut vein of the sun
That shed goldmotes by the million
Against a boy's bare toe foot ankle knee.

Then when the old year fell out of the window
To break into snowflakes on the cold stones of City Hall
I discovered Tennyson in a secondhand bookstore;
He put his bugle for me to his bearded mouth,
And down his Aquitaine nose a diminutive King Arthur
Rode out of our grocery shop bowing to left and to right,
Bearing my mother's *sheitel* with him;
And for a whole week after that
I called my cat Launcelot.

Now I look out for the evil retinue
Making their sortie out of a forest of gold;
Afterwards their dames shall weave my *tzitzith*
Into a tapestry,
Though for myself I had preferred
A death by water or sky.

# DEATH OF MOISHE LAZAROVITCH

My father's coffin pointed me to this:
O arrogant with new life his black beard
Fierce and stiff and partner to the dark wood
Sent me the way to what I most had feared

Became at the last a ring of bright light,
A well whose wall of mourning faces turned
My sighs to silence to a deep wound
Which stained the outstretched figure as it burned.

I swear it burned! If not, why the bright light
Like a tall post that had caught the sun's ray?
White the figure was and bright O so bright,
I have not seen its equal since that day.

I do not know how they lifted him up
Or held the vessel near their mourning silk,
But their going was like a roar of flames
And Matter sang in my ears like poured milk.

# SEVEN O'CLOCK LECTURE

Filling their ears
With the immortal claptrap of poetry,
These singular lies with the power
    to get themselves believed,
The permanent bloom on all time-infected things;
Indicating the will to falsehood in the hearts of men,
The music in a pismire's walk, the necessary glory of dung,
    immortal coal of the universe,
Leibniz's mirroring monads, daybeams of consciousness

I see their heads sway at the seven o'clock lecture;
I imagine they forget the hungers, the desperate fears
    in the hollow parts of their bodies,
The physiological smells, the sardine cans, the flitch of bacon,
The chicken bones gathered neatly
                to one side of the plate;
Life is horrifying, said Cézanne,
                        but this is not
    what he meant who picked flowers blooming
    in the slaughterhouse; he meant the slit throats,
The bear traps smeared with blood, the iron goads,
    the frightened
        servant-girl's Caesarian,
And this planet dancing about Apollo,
    the blood drying and shining in the sun,
Turning to Titians, beauty, the Arts. . . .

My heart is parted like the Red Sea.
It cracks!
And where the cleft is formed
The BARBARI carrying their chromium gods
    on their sunburnt arms and shoulders
Ride on my nightmares, a hot desert wind
    pushing them swiftly toward these faces
    washed clean of Death and Agony;

God! God! Shall I jiggle my gored haunches
    to make these faces laugh?
Shall the blood rain down on these paper masks?
Flammonde, Light of the World, in this well-lit
    fluorescent age you are a failure, lacking savvy;
Gregor Metamorphosis, fantastic bogeylouse,
        you are without meaning to those who nightly
        bed down on well-aired sheets;
In the fifth row someone pulls out a laundered emotion
    and wipes his long, false nose.

At last the bell goes, Lear lamenting Cordelia, the wall's
    piercing cry. . . .

        You may grieve now, gentlemen.


**GOLFERS**


Like Sieur Montaigne's distinction
between virtue and innocence
what gets you is their unbewilderment

They come into the picture suddenly
like unfinished houses, gapes and planed wood,
dominating a landscape

And you see at a glance
among sportsmen they are the metaphysicians,
intent, untalkative, pursuing Unity

(What finally gets you is their chastity)

And that no theory of pessimism is complete
which altogether ignores them

## CAT DYING IN AUTUMN

I put the cat outside to die,
Laying her down
Into a rut of leaves
Cold and bloodsoaked;
Her moan
Coming now more quiet
And brief in October's economy
Till the jaws
Opened and shut on no sound.

Behind the wide pane
I watched the dying cat
Whose fur like a veil of air
The autumn wind stirred
Indifferently with the leaves:
Her form (or was it the wind?)
Still breathing –
A surprise of white.

And I was thinking
Of melting snow in spring
Or a strip of gauze
When a sparrow
Dropped down beside it
Leaning his clean beak
Into the hollow;
Then whirred away, his wings,
You may suppose, shuddering.

Letting me see
From my house
The twisted petal
That fell
Between the ruined paws
To hold or play with,
And the tight smile
Cats have for meeting death.

## FOR MUSIA'S GRANDCHILDREN

I write this poem
for your grandchildren
for they will know of your loveliness
only from hearsay,
from yellowing photographs
spread out on table and sofa
for a laugh.

When arrogant
with the lovely grace you gave their flesh
they regard your dear frail body pityingly,
your time-dishonoured cheeks
pallid and sunken
and those hands
that I have kissed a thousand times
mottled by age
and stroking a grey ringlet into place,
I want them suddenly
to see you as I saw you
– beautiful as the first bird at dawn.

Dearest love, tell them
that I, a crazed poet all his days
who made woman
his ceaseless study and delight,
begged but one boon
in this world of mournful beasts
that are almost human:
to live praising your marvellous eyes
mischief could make glisten
like winter pools at night
or appetite put a fine finish on.

# THE HAUNTING

Why without cease do I think of a bold youth
   national origin unimportant or racial Peruvian
Russian Irish Javanese he has fine clear eyes
honest smiling mouth a pat for a child's head
talks to old women and helps them cross the street
   is friendly with mainliners anarchs and nuns
Cote St. Luc housewives their ruined husbands and brats
optometrists sign painters lumpenproletarians dumping
their humps into coffee cups plotting revenge
and clerics who've made out of Christ a bearded faggot

From the rotating movement of a girl's beautiful
   buttocks he draws energy as from the sun
(O lovely revolving suns on St. Catherine street)
and from breasts and perfumed shoulders and hair
Piccadilly Wilhelmstrasse Fifth Avenue Rue St. Germain
   the suns go rolling on luminous hoops pinwheels
handsprings and somersaults of desirable flesh
the bold youth with wide-apart happy eyes
stepping lightly over blossoming asphalt graves is running
after them touching a child's head smiling to old women

Why don't I ever meet him face to face?
   sometimes I've seen him stepping off a bus
but when I've caught up with him he's changed
into a bourgeois giving the two-fingered peace sign
or a poet shouting love as if it were a bomb
   on damp days into an office clerk smelling of papers
is he somebody's doppelganger? an emanation or
shadow I see taking shape near a plateglass window?
who is he? he haunts me like an embodied absence
and as if I had lived all my life in arrears

# END OF THE WHITE MOUSE

I do not know what Chinese dragons eat
but *vipera russellii* in cages must be fed

On the soft mat of vipershit, godlike,
without compassion or malice
the famed nutritionist
released the white mouse
– cotton fluff with bright pink eyes –
and for a second only
the poor albino
turned to us his bewildered pink eyes
then shifted and ran around the cage
– the dancing, prancing little show-off;
ran with the heady stuff of life
in his ridiculous tiny wishbone legs,
at times raising himself against the glass cage,
standing there, white, like a splayed bat,
then fluttering off into the flecked shadows,
a piece of cambric in a sudden lift of air

Stung,
the white mouse reared up,
swayed and wobbled like a diapered infant
– the death quiver in his small buttocks –
then fell like a furred stone,
the four legs stiffening with eternity

The unhinged viper
swallowed him head first
and the last I saw of the mouse
was a poignant good-bye flick of his tail,
the soothing peristalsis
ending only when he rested
in the middle of the viper's length:
a pleasant, elastic, cosy bubble
lulling as the Madonna's lap after the Annunciation

And I broke into laughter
for this absurdity
and for the mouse's juices soon to begin
running the length and roundness of the viper,
for the flesh and fragile bones commencing
their inevitable transformative cellular dance

I laughed
as might any well-disciplined Zarathustrian
in this godless epoch
but that evening after I'd sown grass seed
in the round bald spot of my lawn
neatly circular as Caesar's empty pate,
restored the earth and watered it carefully,
suddenly when I was resting on the doorstep
I felt a tremor in my head and frame
as if a whole world had moved inside me


## OSIP MANDELSHTAM (1891-1940)


I once did an hour-long TV show reading
from your *Stamen* and *Tristia:* out there
were my compatriots who had never before
heard of your name and pain, your nightmare fate;
of course the impressario spoke impressively
about your stay in Paris where you mastered
the French symbolists, your skill as translator
(what pre-Belsen Jew hadn't promiscuously
shacked up with five or six gentile cultures)
the Hellenic feeling in your prose and poems
– to be brief, he filled in the familiar picture
of enlightened Jew ass bared to the winds

But when that self-taught master symbolist
il miglior fabbro put you on his list of touchables
that was the end; you perished in the land waste
of Siberia, precisely where no one knows and few care
for in that stinking imperium whose literature
you adorned like a surrealist Star of David
you're still an unclaimed name, a Jewish ghost
who wanders occasionally into enclaves
of forlorn intellectuals listening
for the ironic scrape of your voice
in the subversive hum of underground presses

I know my fellow-Canadians, Osip;
they forgot your name and fate as swiftly
as they learned them, switching off
the contorted image of pain with their sets,
choosing a glass darkness to one which starting
in the mind covers the earth in permanent eclipse;
so they chew branflakes and crabmeat gossip make love
take out insurance against fires and death
while our poetesses explore their depressions
in delicate complaints regular as menstruation
or eviscerate a dead god for metaphors;
the men-poets displaying codpieces of wampum,
the safer legends of prairie Indian and Eskimo

Under a sour and birdless heaven
TV crosses stretch across a flat Calvary
and plaza storewindows give me
the blank expressionless stare of imbeciles:
this is Toronto, not St. Petersburg on the Neva;
though seas death and silent decades separate us
we yet speak to each other, brother to brother;
your forgotten martyrdom has taught me scorn
for hassidic world-savers without guns and tanks:
they are mankind's gold and ivory toilet bowls
where brute or dictator relieves himself
when reading their grave messages to posterity
– let us be the rapturous eye of the hurricane
flashing the Jew's will, his mocking contempt for slaves

# TERRORISTS

Insulted, forsaken exiles
harried, harassed, shat on
learning
        Justice is heard only
when it speaks through the mouth
of a cannon

learning
        Right lies waiting
to fly out of a gun barrel

learning weakness is the one crime
history never pardons or condones

Uselessly you bruise yourselves, squirming
against civilization's whipping post;
Black September wolfcubs
terrify only themselves

The Jewish terrorists, ah:
Maimonides, Spinoza, Freud,
Marx

The whole world is still quaking

## BODHIDHARMA

From what sputtering taper
was my light kindled
. . . to sputter in its turn

Detached iotas of flame
fall into the Vast Emptiness
to turn up fragments of poems
floating on its nearest facet.
I roar with furious laughter.

My pleasure in discomfiting
enemies and friends alike
is a gift from the Gautama himself.

And where I turn
I meet myself
striding the other way.

At sudden moments
power can come flooding in
from unseen major stars, from geese
and leaping goats
to soak all my follicles
in the sweetness of Buddhi.

That's why my face
looks like a clenched fist
and I am always irascible.

## SAINT PINCHAS

You sit bolt upright as if you want to know
Why so many crowd to kiss your Jewish toe;
Why gaunt acolytes, why prelates wearing stoles
Rub their pious hair-dos under your worn-out sole
And all file reverently before your feet
To move their hungering lips as if they would eat
While in every procession the more devout
Struggle to finger the metal toe-jam out.
Kissing or smelling the stale dust they press
A breezy crucifix and bowing low bless
The gold air around them, themselves most of all,
Grateful they have not fallen despite the Fall.
Pinchas, your rubbed, much-patted, much-smacked toes shine
With a radiance your brother made divine
Though to kindred Jews it seems the big one glows
Bright and secular like W. C. Fields' nose
And if you could would at once raise it to poke
The eyes out of these stupid credulous folk
And with Jewish sardony plant a neat kick
In the wet mouth of that black-gowned tonsured wick
Who scans my girl when he's left off kissing your toe
As if he'd like to sport with her an hour or so,
Make in his confessional the two-backed beast
Chomp on her nipples and on her vulva feast.
The dumbfounded expression on your face
Here in this basilica seems quite in place
As though it was wanting all your brazen art
To stiffly sit on a wild redundant fart
So propelling it might make your figure rise
Before their delighted superstitious eyes:
My dear silly Pinchas, stunned you look as though
You had heard again the cock's first rending crow.

*Saint Peter's Basilica,*
*June 4, 1975*

# DENNIS LEE

## 400: COMING HOME

You are still on the highway and the great light of
noon comes over the asphalt, the gravelled
shoulders. You are on the highway, there is a kind of
laughter, the cars pound
south. Over your shoulder the scrub-grass, the fences,
the fields wait patiently as though someone
believed in them. The light has laid it
upon them. One
crow scrawks. The edges
take care of themselves, there is
no strain, you can almost hear it, you
inhabit it.

Back in the city many things you lived for
are coming apart.
Transistor rock still fills
back yards, in the parks young men do things to
hondas; there will be
heat lightning, beer on the porches, goings on.
That is not it.

And you are still on the highway. There are no
houses, no farms. Across the median, past the swish and thud of the
northbound cars, beyond the opposite
fences, the fields, the
climbing escarpment, solitary in the
bright eye of the sun the
birches dance, and they
dance. They have
their reasons. You do not know
anything.
Cicadas call now, in the darkening swollen air there is dust
in your nostrils; a
kind of laughter; you are still on the highway.

# 1838

The Compact sat in parliament
To legalize their fun.
And now they're hanging Sammy Lount
And Captain Anderson.
And if they catch Mackenzie
They will string him in the rain.
And England will erase us if
Mackenzie comes again.

The Bishop has a paper
That says he owns our land.
The Bishop has a Bible too
That says our souls are damned.
Mackenzie had a printing press.
It's soaking in the Bay.
And who will spike the Bishop till
Mackenzie comes again?

The British want the country
For the Empire and the view.
The Yankees want the country for
A yankee barbecue.
The Compact want the country
For their merrie green domain.
They'll all play finders-keepers till
Mackenzie comes again.

Mackenzie was a crazy man,
He wore his wig askew.
He donned three bulky overcoats
In case the bullets flew.
Mackenzie talked of fighting
While the fight went down the drain.
But who will speak for Canada?
Mackenzie, come again!

# THURSDAY

Powerful men can fuck up too. It is Thursday,
a mean old lady has died, she got him his
paper route and there is still that whiff of
ju-jube and doilies from her front hall; a stroke; he can
taste them going soggy; some in his pocket too, they always picked up
lint; anyway, she is dead.
And tonight there are things to do in the study, he has a
report, he has the kids, it is
almost too much. Forty-five years, and
still the point eludes him whenever he stops to think.
Next morning,
hacking the day into shape on the phone, there is still no
way – routine & the small ache,
he cannot accommodate both.
At Hallowe'en too, in her hall.
And I know which one he takes and that
night at six, while the kids are tackling his legs with their small tussling,
how he fends them off, tells them "Play upstairs"; one day
they will be dead also with their jelly beans.
In her kitchen, she had a parrot that said "Down the hatch!"

## CIVIL ELEGY 5
*(In Nathan Phillips Square, City Hall, Toronto)*


It would be better maybe if we could stop loving the children
and their delicate brawls, pelting across the square
(In Nathan Phillips Square, City Hall, Toronto) in tandem, deking
from cover to cover in raucous celebration and they are never
winded, bemusing us with the rites of our own
gone childhood; if only they stopped
mattering, the children, it might be possible, now
while the square lies stunned by noon.
What is real is fitful, and always the beautiful footholds
crumble the moment I set my mind aside, though the world does recur.
Better, I think, to avoid the scandal of being – the headlong particulars
which as they lose their animal purchase
cease to endorse us, though the ignominious hankering
goes on; this awakens the ache of being, and the lonesome ego
sets out once again dragging its lethal desires across the world,
which does not regard them.
Perhaps we should
bless what doesn't attach us, though I do not know
where we are to find nourishment.
So, in the square, it is a
blessed humdrum; the kids climb over the Archer, and
the pool reflects the sky, and the people passing by,
who doze, and gently from above the visible pollutants descend,
coating the towers' sheath. Sometimes it
works but once in summer looking up I saw the noxious cloud suspended
taut above the city, clenched, as now everywhere it is the
imperial way of life that bestows its fallout. And it did not
stay inert, but across the fabled horizon of Bay Street they came riding,
the liberators, the deputies of Jesus, the Marines, and had released
bacterial missiles over the Golden Horseshoe for love of all mankind,
and I saw my people streaming after calling welcome for the small
    change,
and I ran in my mind crying humiliation upon the country, as now I do
    also for it is
hard to stay at the centre when you're losing it one more time,
although the pool
reflects the placid sky, and the people passing by, and daily
our acquiescence presses down on us from above and we have no room
    to be.
It is the children's fault as they swarm for we cannot stop caring.

In a bad time, people, from an outpost of empire I write
bewildered, though on about living. It is to set down a nation's
failure of nerve; I mean complicity, which is signified by the
gaseous stain above us. For a man who
fries the skin of kids with burning jelly is a
criminal. Even though he loves children he is a criminal. Even though his
money pumps your oil he is criminal, and though his programs infest the
        air you breathe he is
criminal and though his honest quislings run your
government he is criminal and though you do not love his enemies he is
criminal and though you lose your job on his say-so he is criminal and
though your country will founder without him he is criminal and though
        he has
transformed the categories of your refusal by the pressure of his media he
        is a criminal.
And the consenting citizens of a minor and docile colony
are cogs in a useful tool, though in no way
necessary and scarcely
criminal at all and their leaders are
honourable men, as for example Paul Martin.

In Germany, the civic square in many little towns is
hallowed for people. Laid out just so, with
flowers and fountains and during the war you could come and
relax for an hour, catch a parade or just
get away from the interminable racket of the trains, clattering through the
outskirts with their lousy expendable cargo.
Little cafes often, fronting the square. Beer and a chance to relax.
And except for the children it's peaceful here
too, under the sun's warm sedation.

The humiliations of imperial necessity
are an old story, though it does not
improve in the telling and no man
believes it of himself.
Why bring up genocide? Why bring up
acquiescence, profiteering? Why bring up, again,
the deft emasculation of a country by the Liberal party of Canada?
It was not Mr Martin who sprayed the poison mist
on the fields of the Vietnamese, not in person nor fried civilians – he was
no worse a man than the other sellouts of history:
the Britons who went over to the legionaries, sadly for the sake of the
        larger peace,

the tired professors of Freiburg, Berlin, the statesmen at Munich, those
estimable men, and the lovers of peace, the brisk switchers who
told it in Budapest. Doesn't the
service of quiet diplomacy require dirty hands?
(Does the sun in summer pour its warm light into the square
for us to ignore?)
And then if it doesn't work one is finally
on the winning side – though that is
unkind: Mr Martin was an honourable man, as we are all
Canadians and honourable men.

And this is void, to participate in an
abomination larger than yourself. It is to fashion
other men's napalm and know it, to be a
Canadian safe in the square and watch the children dance and
dance and smell the lissome burning
bodies to be born in
old necessity to breathe polluted air and
come of age in Canada with lies and vertical on earth no man has
　　　　drawn a
breath that was not lethal to some brother it is
yank and gook and hogtown linked in
guilty genesis it is the sorry mortal
sellout burning kids by proxy acquiescent
still though still denying it is merely to be human.

# DOROTHY LIVESAY

## OTHER

1

Men prefer an island
With its beginning ended:
Undertone of waves
Trees overbended.

Men prefer a road
Circling, shell-like
Convex and fossiled
Forever winding inward.

Men prefer a woman
Limpid in sunlight
Held as a shell
On a sheltering island. . . .

Men prefer an island.

2

But I am mainland
O I range
From upper country to the inner core:
From sageland, brushland, marshland
To the sea's floor.

Show me an orchard where I have not slept,
A hollow where I have not wrapped
The sage about me, and above, the still
Stars clustering
Over the ponderosa pine, the cactus hill.

Tell me a time
I have not loved,
A mountain left unclimbed:
A prairie field
Where I have not furrowed my tongue,
Nourished it out of the mind's dark places;
Planted with tears unwept
And harvested as friends, as faces.

O find me a dead-end road
I have not trodden
A logging road that leads the heart away
Into the secret evergreen of cedar roots
Beyond sun's farthest ray –
Then, in a clearing's sudden dazzle,
There is no road; no end; no puzzle.

But do not show me! For I know
The country I caress:
A place where none shall trespass
None possess:
A mainland mastered
From its inaccess.

    * * * *

Men prefer an island.

## BALLAD OF ME

I

Misbegotten
born clumsy
bursting feet first
then topsy turvy
falling downstairs:
the fear of
joy of
falling.

*Butterfingers*
father called it
throwing the ball
which catch as catch can
I couldn't.

Was it the eyes' fault
seeing the tennis net
in two places?
the ball flying, falling
space-time team-up?

What happened was:
the world, chuckling sideways
tossed me off
left me wildly
treading air
to catch up.

II

Everyone expected guilt
even I –
the pain was this:
to feel nothing.

Guilt? for the abortionist
who added one more line
to his flat perspective
one more cloud of dust
to his bleary eye?

For the child's
'onlie begetter'
who wanted a daughter?
He'll make another.

For the child herself
the abortive dancer?

No. Not for her
no tears.
I held the moon in my belly
nine months' duration
then she burst forth
an outcry of poems.

## III

*And what fantasies do you have?*
asked the psychiatrist
when I was running away from my husband.
Fantasies? fantasies?
Why surely (I might have told him)
all this living
is just that
every day dazzled
gold coins falling
                through fingers.
So I emptied my purse for the doctor
See!   nothing in it
but wishes.
He sent me back home
to wash dishes.

## IV

Returning further now
to childhood's *Woodlot*
I go incognito
in sandals, slacks
old sweater
and my dyed
hair

I go disarrayed
my fantasies
twist in my arms
ruffle my hair

I go wary
fearing to scare
the crow

        No one remembers Dorothy
        was ever here.

## THE UNINVITED

Always a third one's there
where any two are walking out
along a river-bank    so mirror-still
sheathed in sheets    of sky
pillows of cloud –
their footprints crunch the hardening earth
their eyes delight in trees    stripped clean
winter-prepared
with only the rose-hips red
and the plump fingers of sumach

And always between the two
(scuffing the leaves, laughing
and fingers locked)
goes a third lover    his or hers
who walked this way with one or other    once
flung back the head    snapped branches of dark pine
in armfuls    before snowfall

      I walk beside you
      trace
      a shadow's shade
      skating on silver
      hear
      another voice
      singing under ice

## SEASHELTER

The houses last longer
than those who lived there
who hammered 2 by 4's
wainscotted, plastered walls
unfrantically
painted them pink or blue
(never a green wall)

This shingle house was made
high on a mountain
                    when the crew went in
to heave and haul
                    the forest
tame it down
with donkey engine
then the stripped bark
and logs rolled
lumbering   down
                    (the land left bleeding)

When they cleared out they hoisted houses high
on sledges over barren forest rubble
and tumbled them to the sea
to be towed down to the quiet beaches
Porpoise Bay
and landed.

House weather-stained
with leaking roof
        wind-beaten
            water-soaked
house lived in
        locked box where
I saw your faded photograph
in an old trunk

The cracking walls
still stood –
but you
had gone.

# GWENDOLYN MacEWEN

## THE BREAKFAST

under the knuckles of the warlord sun how long do we have
how long do we have, you ask, in the vast magenta wastes
of the morning world when the bone buckles under for war
when the bone intersects as tangent in the district of the sun
centipedes and infidels; snakes and the absence of doves?

a breakfast hysteria; perhaps you have felt it,
the weight of the food you eat, the end of the meal coming
before you lift the spoon; or eat only apples
to improvise an eden, or forget the end takes place
in each step of your function.

look, the spoon is lifted halfway through invisible tables
of dangerous logarithms in the abstract morning spaces;
come, come – eat leviathans in the breakfast wastelands,
eat bestiaries and marine zoos and apples and aviaries.
by eating the world you may enclose it.

seek simplicities; the fingerprints of the sun only
and the fingernails of the moon duplicating you in your body
the cosmos meets your measures, has no ending.

place one hand before the sun and make it smaller,
hold the spoon in your hand up to the sky
and marvel at its relative size; comfort yourself
with the dimensions of a momentary breakfast table.

ah lord sun
ah terrible atomic breakfast
ah twilight of purple fallout
ah last deck of evening cards –

deal, infidel, the night is indeed difficult

# THE GARDEN OF SQUARE ROOTS: AN AUTOBIOGRAPHY

and then the rattlesnake spines of men distracted me
for even they, the people were
as Natajara was, who danced
while I was anchored like a passive verb
or Neptune on a subway –

and from the incredible animal i
grew queer claws inward to fierce cribs;
I searched gardens for square roots,
for i was the I interior
the thing with a gold belt and delicate ears
with no knees or elbows
was working from the inside out

this city I live in I built with bones
and mortared with marrow;
I planned it in my spare time
and its hydro is charged from a blood niagara
and I built this city backwards and
the people evolved out of the buildings
and the subway uterus ejected them –

for i was the I interior
the thing with a gold belt and delicate ears
with no knees or elbows
was working from the inside out.

and all my gardens grew backwards
and all the roots were finally square
and Ah! the flowers grew there like algebra

# THE THING IS VIOLENT

Self, I want you now to be
violent and without history,
for we've rehearsed too long our ceremonial ballet
and I fear my calm against your exquisite rage.

I do not fear that I will go mad
but that I may not, and the shadows of my sanity
blacken out your burning; act once
and you need not act again –
give me no ceremony, scars are not pain.

The thing is violent, nothing precedes it,
it has no meaning before or after –
sweet wounds which burn like stars,
stigmata of the self's own holiness,
appear and plot new zodiacs upon the flesh.

# LETTER TO A FUTURE GENERATION

we did not anticipate you, you bright ones
though some of us saw you kneeling behind our bombs,
we did not fervently grow towards you
for most of us grew backwards
sowing our seed in the black fields of history

avoid monuments, engrave our names beneath your own
for you have consumed our ashes by now
for you have one quiet mighty language by now

do not excavate our cities
to catalogue the objects of our doom
but burn all you find to make yourselves room,
you have no need of archaeology,
your faces are your total history

for us it was necessary to invent a darkness,
to subtract light in order to see,
for us it was certain death to know our names
as they were written in the black books of history

I stand with an animal at my left hand
and a warm, breathing ghost at my right
saying, Remember that this letter was made
for you to burn, that its meaning lies
only in your burning it,
that its lines await your cleansing fire –
understand it only insofar
as that warm ghost at my right hand breathed
down my blood and for a moment wrote the lines
while guns sounded out from a mythical city
and destroyed the times

# THE CHILD DANCING

there's no way I'm going to write about
the child dancing in the Warsaw ghetto
in his body of rags

there were only two corpses
on the pavement that day
and the child I will not write about
had a face as pale and trusting
as the moon

(so did
the boy with a green belly full of dirt
lying by the roadside
in a novel of Kazantzakis
and the small girl T. E. Lawrence wrote about
who they found after the Turkish massacre
with one shoulder chopped off, crying:
"don't *hurt* me, Baba!")

I don't feel like slandering them with poetry.

the child who danced
in the Warsaw ghetto
to some music no one else could hear
had moon-eyes, no
green horror and no fear
but something worse

a simple desire to please
the people who stayed
to watch him shuffle back and forth,
his feet wrapped in the newspapers
of another ordinary day

## PRUNE

was a huge totally worthless and basically hideous old grey
cat who died

everything dies and I'll get God for that

I might even get God for the manner of this death

because Prune who was grey and hopeless had to
drag half of his paralyzed body across the floor
dripping blood and slime all over
the place

dripping death into his shit-box and keeling over
and lying there

his head resting neatly on his last stool


## WATCH ME

Watch me
I am moving through the cages of the animals
I am moving through the peereek of their cells
Watch me because
I am watching them watching you
They are holding your immortal souls in trust
They have watched you since Eden
They are waiting for their time

# JAY MacPHERSON

## EVE IN REFLECTION

Painful and brief the act. Eve on the barren shore
Sees every cherished feature, plumed tree, bright grass,
Fresh spring, the beasts as placid as before
Beneath the inviolable glass.

There the lost girl gone under sea
Tends her undying grove, never raising her eyes
To where on the salt shell beach in reverie
The mother of all living lies.

The beloved face is lost from sight,
Marred in a whelming tide of blood:
And Adam walks in the cold night
Wilderness, waste wood.

## EURYNOME

Come all old maids that are squeamish
And afraid to make mistakes,
Don't clutter your lives up with boyfriends:
The nicest girls marry snakes.

If you don't mind slime on your pillow
And caresses as gliding as ice
– Cold skin, warm heart, remember,
And besides, they keep down the mice –

If you're really serious-minded,
It's the best advice you can take:
No rumpling, no sweating, no nonsense,
Oh who would not sleep with a snake?

# THE PLOWMAN IN DARKNESS

You ask for the Plowman:
He's as much
In the dark as you are,
Moves by touch,
Stubbing his toes
From age to age
Is working up a
Snorting rage,
Swears he'll beat his plowshare
Into a sword
Come the great and harrowing
Day of the Lord.

# THE MARTYRS

The sexes waking, now separate and sore,
Enjoy conjunction not feasible before;
But never long enough, never near enough, nor yet
Find their death mortal, however deeply met.

Bound to cross-purposes, transfixed with desire,
His raw heart unsheltered behind its broken wall,
The first martyr bleeds impaled upon the briar
Whose root is pleasure's spring, whose arms are sorrow's fall.

The woman meanwhile sits apart and weaves
Red rosy garlands to dress her joy and fear.
But all to no purpose; for petals and leaves
Fall everlastingly, and the small swords stand clear.

## THE UNICORN-TREE

Bound and weeping, but with smiles
To keep herself from scorn,
The lady of the tree beguiles
The wrathful unicorn.

What anger in the springing wood
Or coil along the bough
Flushes the milky skin with blood?
Too late to question now.

The hunters with their kill are gone.
The darkening tree again
Arches its wicked length upon
The virgin in her chain.

## STORM

That strong creature   from before the Flood,
headless, sightless,   without bone or blood,
a wandering voice,   a travelling spirit,
butting to be born,   fierce to inherit
acreage of pity,   the world of love,
the Christian child's kingdom,   and remove
the tall towered gates   where the proud sea lay
crouched on its paws   in the first day –
came chaos again,   that outsider
would ride in,   blind steed, blind rider:
till then wails at windows,   denies relief,
batters the body   in speechless grief,
thuds in the veins,   crumples in the bone,
wrestles in darkness   and alone
for kingdoms cold,   for salt, sand, stone,
forever dispossessed.
                Who raised this beast,
this faceless angel,   shall give him rest.

## LIKE ADAMANT

I thought there was no second Fall,
That I with Eve fell once for all:
But worse succeeds, I no more doubt,
Since heaven-dwellers make me out
First fallen, last obstructive grown,
Like Adamant the wounded stone.

For Adamant with Adam fell
From diamond clear to black as hell,
Though not from heaven dropped so far
As the imperious angels are,
But lies malignant in the sea,
Drawing by its infirmity.

Reader, my sound one, why should you
Hate me, or fear what I might do?
Since Adamant, as is well known,
In whom the wounds of love are shown,
Threatens the man of iron alone,
And not the man of flesh, nor stone.


## HECATE TRIVIA

Here in a land of faultless four-leaved clovers,
Learning from books how, back before our windows,
Mirrors, your dusty forks were where uncanny
    Worlds faced each other,

We, where our fathers banished wolf and Indian,
Vainly regret their vanished sense and vigour:
Now in our cities take a last, last stand with
    Rat and with cockroach.

Goddess of crossways, three-faced, was it you my
Muse all this while? you are the last who hallows
Contents of pockets, broken dolls, dead puppies:
    Queen, garbage-eater.

# ELI MANDEL

## NOTES FROM THE UNDERGROUND

A woman built herself a cave
    and furnished it with torn machines
    and tree-shaped trunks and dictionaries
Out of the town where she sprang
    to her cave of rusting texts and springs
    rushed fables of indifferent rape
    and children slain indifferently
    and daily blood.

Would you believe how free I have become
    with lusting after her?
                That I have become
a melodramatist, my friends ashamed?

I have seen by the light of her burning texts
    how the indifferent blood drips
    from the brass mouths of my friends,
    how at the same table I will eat
    and grow fat.

Her breasts are planets in a reedy slough.
Lie down beside that slough awhile
    and taste the bitter reed.

Read in the water how a drowning man
    sings of a free green life.

# SONG

When the echo of the last footstep dies
and on the empty street you turn your empty eyes,
what do you think you will see?
A hangman and a hanging tree.

When there are no more voices
and yet you hear voices singing
in the hot street,
what do you think will be their song?
Glory to the hangman who is never wrong.

When on the hot sands of your burning mind
iron footsteps clang no more
and blind eyes no longer see
and voices end,
what do you think will be your plea?
Hanging isn't good enough for me.

# DAVID

all day the gopher-killing boys
  their sling-shot arms
    their gopher-cries

the king insisting
  my poetry must stop

I have written nothing since May

instead
      walk among the boys
gopher-blood on their stretched
hands
      murder will end murder
the saying goes, someone must
do something about the rodents
and poems do not:
          even the doctors
admit that it's plague
ask me about my arms
        look
at my shadow hanging
  like a slingshot

the world turns like a murderous stone
  my forehead aching with stars

## GIRL ON A HIGH WIRE

Do you think I'd sit here staring
if I knew how to work a chair-lift
or lacked this odd taste for vertigo?

What if I dare you to jump, saying, ah
my hurt bird, I will catch you –
and if I weren't there (someone calling,
my son pointing at camels or wanting
to pee) when your eyes became horizons?
Or if you fell
into the well of bankers, mid-wives,
my brother-in-law, the Prudential Life
Insurance Company?
                           I see them,
heroine, hefting you, their applause
ringing your head with the clatter of zircons,
mouths blowing little balloons of praise.

The great globe circles.
Soldiers fall into muddy rivers.
Boys walk the tightrope of their prison yard.

I can no longer look at telephone wires,
the vanishing point of your unfinished portrait.

I shall devote myself to entomology,
practise weight-lifting with dinky toys,
but who will keep me from my crooked prayers,
those mad doves that fling haloes around you?

## PSALM 24

What did you expect?
You, who drove me to mad alphabets
and taught me all the wrong words.

Isn't it enough that I've failed?

It's your scripture. You read it.

## ESTEVAN, 1934

remembering the family we
called breeds   the Roques
their house smelling of urine
my mother's prayers before
the dried fish she cursed
them for their dirtiness their
women I remember too
                        how
seldom they spoke and
they touched one another

even when the sun killed
cattle and rabbis
                even
in the poisoned slow air
like hunters
            like lizards
they touched   stone
they touched
                earth

# JOHN NEWLOVE

## THE DOUBLE-HEADED SNAKE

Not to lose the feel of the mountains
while still retaining the prairies
is a difficult thing. What's lovely
is whatever makes the adrenalin run;
therefore I count terror and fear among
the greatest beauty. The greatest
beauty is to be alive, forgetting nothing,
although remembrance hurts
like a foolish act, is a foolish act.

Beauty's whatever
makes the adrenalin run. Fear
in the mountains at night-time's
not tenuous, it is not the cold
that makes me shiver, civilized man,
white, I remember
the stories of the Indians,
Sis-i-utl, the double-headed snake.

Beauty's what makes
the adrenalin run. Fear at night
on the level plains, with no horizon
and the stars too bright, wind bitter
even in June, in winter
the snow harsh and blowing,
is what makes me
shiver, not the cold air alone.

And one beauty cancels another. The plains
seem secure and comfortable
at Crow's Nest Pass; in Saskatchewan
the mountains are comforting
to think of; among
the eastwardly diminishing hills
both the flatland and the ridge
seem easy to endure.

As one beauty
cancels another, remembrance
is a foolish act, a double-headed snake
striking in both directions, but I
remember plains and mountains, places
I come from, places I adhere and live in.

# DOUKHOBOR

When you die and your weathery corpse
lies on the chipped kitchen table,

the wind blowing the wood of your house
painted in shades of blue, farmer

out from Russia as the century turned,
died, and lay at the feet of the wars,

who will ever be able to say for you
what you thought at the sight of the Czar's horsemen

riding with whips among you, the sight
of the rifles burning in bonfires,

the long sea-voyage, strange customs endured,
officials changing your name

into the strange script that covered the stores,
the polite brown men who spoke no language

you understood and helped you
free your team from Saskatchewan river mud,

who will be able to say for you
just what you thought as the villages marched

naked to Eden and the English
went to war and came back again

with their funny ways, proud
to speak of killing each other, you, whose mind

refused the slaughter, refused the blood,
you who will lie in your house, stiff as winter,

dumb as an ox, unable to love,
while your women sob and offer the visitors tea?

## THE CAVE

The stars are your death-bed.
You rest from the cave
to Pluto or whatever dark planets
lie beyond. No ideas trap you.

In the unobstructed sunlight miles high
the Earth is beautiful as a postcard.
Sinai looks as the map says it should,
and people are too small to be observed.

In Africa there are no trees to see.
It is a map world.
The sunlight is brilliant
as a two-carat diamond on a girl's hand.

The girl is young, visible to your mind,
growing older. Beyond Pluto
and the darkest planets, children surround her.

The diamond glows on her finger
like a worm. The stars, the stars
shine like one-carat diamonds. Beyond
Pluto and the darkest planets the stars shine.

The diamonds shine in wormy rings
on fingers, in coffins of unobstructed space.
The flesh circles the bone in strips
in the coffin as the ring circled flesh.

The two-carat sun hangs loosely,
just restraining the Earth. Beyond the planets,
beyond the dark coffin, beyond the ring of stars,
your bed is in the shining, tree-lit cave.

## THE HERO AROUND ME

Water submissive and cool, the abundant sun
hot on my white back, day
of quiet pleasures, air humming
a steady soothing tune through the long hours,
ghosts slowly drifting past,
heads like broad arrows, hair coiled
about faces. Time is sliding away. . . .

I have desired many
but I wonder if I have loved one? –
remembering the cruel amusement and pleasure
of a youth called hard-hearted, ,
joy in a tearful eye and a frantic manner,
dismissive joy, and the day
humming and sliding away. . . .

Once heroes marched through my mind
in solid ranks, the deeds
shaped pointedly, and I knew
I could never be one of them,
though I desired it, wished for one sharp moment
in my life – thinking
of the hero as man in combat only. . . .

The day came, but not as war.
Fields of grain around me were crystal,
the sky polished, endless gold and blue,
and in the still heat a meadowlark
twisted its sculptured tune around me
once, quickly, a deft feat of superior magic,
and all time stopped, world without end,
and I was as a tree is, loathing no one.

# B. P. NICHOL

## THE TRUE EVENTUAL STORY OF BILLY THE KID

this is the true eventual story of billy the kid. it is not the story as he told it for he did not tell it to me. he told it to others who wrote it down, but not correctly. there is no true eventual story but this one. had he told it to me i would have written a different one. i could not write the true one had he told it to me.

this is the true eventual story of the place in which billy died. dead, he let others write his story, the untrue one. this is the true story of billy & the town in which he died & why he was called a kid and why he died. eventually all other stories will appear untrue beside this one.

## 1 – THE KID

billy was born with a short dick but they did not call him richard.

billy might've grown up in a town or a city. it does not matter. the true story is that billy grew & his dick didn't. sometimes he called it a penis or a prick but still it didn't grow. as he grew he called others the same thing & their pricks & penises were big & heavy as dictionaries but his dick remained – short for richard.

billy was not fast with words so he became fast with a gun. they called him the kid so he became faster & meaner. they called him the kid because he was younger & meaner & had a shorter dick.

could they have called him instead billy the man or bloody bonney? would he have bothered having a faster gun? who can tell. the true eventual story is billy became the faster gun. that is his story.

## 2 – HISTORY

history says that billy the kid was a coward. the true eventual story is that billy the kid is dead or he'd probably shoot history in the balls. history always stands back calling people cowards or failures.

legend says that billy the kid was a hero who liked to screw. the true eventual story is that were billy the kid alive he'd probably take legend out for a drink, match off in the bathroom, then blow him full of holes. legend always has a bigger dick than history and history has a bigger dick than billy had.

rumour has it that billy the kid never died. rumour is billy the kid. he never gets anywhere, being too short-lived.

## 3 – THE TOWN

the town in which billy the kid died is the town in which billy the kid killed his first man. he shot him in the guts & they spilled out onto the street like bad conversation. billy did not stand around & talk. he could not be bothered.

the true eventual story is that the man billy killed had a bigger dick. billy was a bad shot & hit him in the guts. this bothered billy. he went out into the back yard & practiced for months. then he went and shot the dick off everyone in sight.

the sheriff of the town said billy, billy why you such a bad boy. and billy said sheriff i'm sick of being the kid in this place. the sheriff was understanding. the sheriff had a short dick too, which was why he was sheriff & not out robbing banks. these things affect people differently.

the true eventual story is billy & the sheriff were friends. if they had been more aware they would have been lovers. they were not more aware. billy ran around shooting his mouth off, & the dicks off everybody else, & the sheriff stood on the sidelines cheering. this is how law & order came to the old west.

## 4 – WHY

when billy died everyone asked why he'd died. and billy said he was sorry but it was difficult to speak with his mouth full of blood. people kept asking him anyway. billy hated small talk so he closed his eyes & went up to heaven. god said billy why'd you do all those things & billy said god my dick was too short. so god said billy i don't see what you're talking about which made billy mad. if billy had had a gun he'd've shot god full of holes.

the true eventual story is that billy the kid shot it out with himself. there was no-one faster. he snuck up on himself & shot himself from behind the grocery store. as he lay dying he said to the sheriff goodbye & the sheriff said goodbye. billy had always been a polite kid. everyone said too bad his dick was so small, he was the true eventual kid.

### LOST ANGLES

let us put this in focus
let us understand why

anger is as sudden as as

young dreams   older fears
the nearness of you
likely as not nearly new

mostly old catalogues
lists
liable to capsize

sudden

holden &
well
     yes
        collapse as

as likely nearly not new

●

something is old as nothing

nearly yearly the millennium come round again

fourths of a moment
airy pleasure
gone

to what gain
to whit
        none
known or un
the wise


●


threading send
or then
        hover
which is lover on
the rind the
pit of it

alpha beta
game as the next one
man i mean

oh i wish these lines were longer longer
the music you can hear
familiar river

# ALDEN NOWLAN

## I, ICARUS

There was a time when I could fly. I swear it.
Perhaps, if I think hard for a moment, I can even tell you the year.
My room was on the ground floor at the rear of the house.
My bed faced a window.
Night after night I lay on my bed and willed myself to fly.
It was hard work, I can tell you.
Sometimes I lay perfectly still for an hour before I felt
    my body rising from the bed.
I rose slowly, slowly until I floated three or four feet
    above the floor.
Then, with a kind of swimming motion, I propelled myself
    toward the window.
Outside, I rose higher and higher, above the pasture fence,
    above the clothesline, above the dark, haunted trees
    beyond the pasture.
And, all the time, I heard the music of flutes.
It seemed the wind made this music.
And sometimes there were voices singing.

## THE SPY

My child cries out in his sleep.
I bend close, try to make out the words.
Though it fills me with shame,
I spy on his dreams,
try each word like a key
to the room where he keeps
things too private to share
even with me.

## THE CHANGELING

Today he told me the story again.
This time the parents lived in the next county.
He gave me their names. Last time they were movie stars.
*Never think it to look at that yellow hair of hers.*
Once or twice, they've been royalty.

She is always as blue
and golden and white
as the longest day of the summer.
*She didn't know it herself until they showed her the baby.*

And afterwards she goes mad
and drinks lysol or shoves her head in an oven.


## THE DARK COMPANIONS

All the physicians say his blood turned black
because in a certain mirror there are laws
that condemn those judged guiltless to go back
to the real world, and break them clause by clause.

Myself, I've dreamt of a great funnel, and
a thousand corpses dump-trucked down its throat,
woke whimpering for light, yet marked the bland
clockwork as one by one it spilled them out.

And I can comprehend how the young boy
in all the papers, watched the stars and thought
of dark companions, his curious joy,
studying his friend's face before he shot.

# REVELATION

This plane does not always travel between Toronto and Vancouver,
    via Edmonton.
Nor do its passengers always wear Chamber of Commerce
    mustaches and expressions of unfathomable boredom.
Sometimes it disappears on mysterious errands
to Tibet and the Middle East, its comings and goings
uncharted even by the International Aeronautics Administration
– though there are rumours, hints in certain old books,
that it was this plane, or another like it,
that landed in Stockholm in 1757
and carried Emanuel Swedenborg
twenty thousand feet into the sky
where he and his fellow passengers
(including that epileptic Arab and that old rabbi from Patmos)
mistook these clouds for an encampment of angels
and the naked sun for the New Jerusalem.


# A BOY IN A RED LOIN CLOTH

He waited for the men to come, and the beautiful white horse
he would ride into the jungle. They would stop by a spring,
where he would bathe and change into a red loin cloth,
and the pygmies would suddenly emerge from the trees
and lead him down the secret road to the city,
beating drums, blowing curious little horns, like fifes
or piccolos – and he would be their prisoner,
(perhaps they would even blindfold him) and there would be elephants
and a great pit full of lions and a sun so big
he could not circle it with his arms, and a house of children
who'd make him their brother, though he was always stronger;
and in time he would leave there, but by then he would know
so many singular arts all men would be awed by him,
    and whenever he wished
he would summon the beautiful white horse and ride back to the jungle.

# X-RAY

Sickness is a crime.
   For habitual offenders
      the penalty is death.
In the doctor's waiting room
   we study one another
      slyly, like embezzlers.
In the hospital
   even those who love us
      seem afraid of what
we might do to them.
   (The sick have no friends.
      Here there are only strangers,
brothers and lovers.)
   Anyone who can walk
      erect without swaying
is my superior.
   Astonishing how soon
      one learns the tricks
the weak use
   against the strong.
      For almost the first time
I have become
   a credible flatterer. Next
      I will learn to whine
– already I find myself
   struggling against it.
      The orderly who sneered
at the fat bearded man
   in the Mother Hubbard –
      would I have done differently
or only been more clever,
   deceiving myself
      that what I felt was pity.

## RE-ENTRY

He has been out of his head
but nowhere else: the diagnosis is delirium.
They have him almost convinced
until he touches
the medallion of the priestess.
    The film ends there.

Sleep is a different story.
    How I fought to keep
every detail of the vision,
a work of art that explained
almost everything!

When I wake up, I thought,
I'll find pencils and scissors and paste and paint
and get all this down
on paper so everyone will perceive
how true and beautiful it is
– a discovery!

Manuscript of an unpublished poem
with a tiny green watercolour
    in the upper right corner
and a drawing of Mark Twain's head
    in the upper left
above a picture
of Little Orphan Annie
    cut from a comic strip.

You see how
the dream dissolves:
    like a fistful of diamonds
that were really ice, after all.

## FIVE DAYS IN HOSPITAL

### 1

I have come beyond fear to a place where there is almost
    silence,
except now I am all the numbers
on all the clocks in the world:
things are broken apart,
I am the ruins of a crystal man
and there are no sentences
but only words. . . .

### 2

I have discovered to my amazement
    that I am unable to believe
        in my own death.
I know that I will die but I do not believe in it.
Then how is it there are times
when I am almost crazy with fear?

### 3

I look IN at the world
like a ghost startled by the sight
of his own body
lying quite apart from him
in this bed. . . .

### 4

Where do flames go when they go out?
    They go back to the sun.
How do they get there?
    Like a flight of birds with bright feathers
        flying south through the black morning. . . .

5

Fear of deafness has stopped my ears.
Fear of blindness has sewn up my eyes.
Fear of nakedness has stripped me bare.
Fear of the desert has made me abjure drink.
Yet even now, bad joke for a black morning,
fear of silence has not stilled my tongue.


## A BLACK PLASTIC BUTTON AND A YELLOW YOYO


I wish I could make her understand
her child isn't the Christ Child
and didn't create the world,
then maybe she'd stop shaking
her fists in his face
and he could come out from inside
his yellow yoyo
or black plastic button
because that's where he hides:
I've watched from my window,
unable to write because of her screaming,
and seen him flying out of his body
into the yoyo,
where he can neither see nor be seen,
neither hear nor speak,
a Buddha smaller than my thumb,
a sleeping Krishna,
there inside that dancing yoyo;
and if she knocks it from his hand,
why, he simply turns
the second button from the top
of his windbreaker,
a black plastic button,
turns it between
his thumb and forefinger,
focuses his eyes on it,
until he is safe again,
curled up in a ball
where nothing at all can reach him.

## O'SULLIVAN'S WORLD

Earth is three billion separate planets
and on one of them
my friend O'Sullivan
tells me there are no women
but only symmetrical
little animals somewhat like deer
that are allowed to go almost anywhere
they like just as cats and pigeons do
in my world and when a man
feels the urge he goes to one of them
with a handful of sugar cubes or if the beast is beautiful
a little ice cream or half of a chocolate bar
and more often than not it trots along beside him
to wherever it is he wants to go,
its tiny hooves beating time to the music
of the clusters of little silver bells
tied with silk ribbons
to its switching tail.

## CORNFLOWERS

I am a saint with a broken wing
   who shakes his fists like the wind.
                               You
are the homecoming
             of the sun,
                      an hurrah of grass.
The cornflowers are not yet
   aware they will die soon
      from last night's frost.
They are like the Empress
Elizabeth of Austria
who was stabbed with a blade so thin
she continued to smile
                 and did not interrupt
her walk,
       although it had pierced her heart.
Since in this place and season
   they are the only flowers
          that do not ask for money
I give you them.
            Nothing else is beautiful
this hunchbacked October night
except the moon.

## LONG AGO AND FAR AWAY

The naked children come out of the lake.
It's as though they lived there.
I am one of them. Now the cherry tree
is full of us, like birds feeding.
We rest at last
in the topmost branches. Below us
our shadows
         dance hand-in-hand
                 with the wind.

# HE PERCEIVES THAT HIS SON IS BECOMING A MAN

Love is nothing I will
but what is done with me.
I would have you stop
like a plucked flower:
                Take care
when I reach out my hand,
                      be cruel if you must,
as I would be if I could.

Nor was it malice
moved the queen
to represent
herself as an apple.

The gift was as it came
from the tree,
it was the giving
proved venomous.

If there are times,
as there have been
and will be,
when love withdraws
for its own reasons,
make such use of them
as you can. Move quickly.
They will not come often.

While I work harder
at my part:
the brain once again
learning to do
what the heart cannot.

**ACT TWO**


She thinks
that which she fears is
behind her, and so
she runs
toward it.
      Worse
it can be dispelled
only by another
and equivalent
act
of the will.
      Next
she will break
through the glass
of the mirror,
screaming.

# MICHAEL ONDAATJE

**AFTER SHOOTING GREGORY**
(from *Billy the Kid*)


After shooting Gregory
this is what happened

I'd shot him well and careful
made it explode under his heart
so it wouldnt last long and
was about to walk away
when this chicken paddles out to him
and as he was falling hops on his neck
digs the beak into his throat
straightens legs and heaves
a red and blue vein out

Meanwhile he fell
and the chicken walked away

still tugging at the vein
till it was 12 yards long
as if it held that body like a kite
Gregory's last words being

get away from me yer stupid chicken

# THE STREET OF THE SLOW MOVING ANIMALS
(from *Billy the Kid*)


The street of the slow moving animals
while the sun drops in perfect verticals
no wider than boots
The dogs sleep their dreams off
they are everywhere
so that horses on the crowded weekend
will step back and snap a leg

/ while I've been going on
the blood from my wrist
has travelled to my heart
and my fingers touch
this soft blue paper notebook
control a pencil that shifts up and sideways
mapping my thinking going its own way
like light wet glasses drifting on polished wood.

The acute nerves spark
on the periphery of our bodies
while the block trunk of us
blunders as if we were
those sun drugged horses

I am here with the range for everything
corpuscle muscle hair
hands that need the rub of metal
those senses that
that want to crash things with an axe
that listen to deep buried veins in our palms
those who move in dreams over your women night
near you, every paw, the invisible hooves
the mind's invisible blackout   the intricate never
the body's waiting rut.

## THE END OF IT, LYING AT THE WALL
(from *Billy the Kid*)


The end of it, lying at the wall
the bullet itch frozen in my head

my right arm is through the window pane
and the cut veins awake me
so I can watch inside and through the window

Garrett's voice going Billy Billy
and the other two dancing circles
saying we got him we got him the little shrunk bugger

the pain at my armpit I'm glad for
keeping me alive at the bone
and suns coming up everywhere out of the walls and floors
Garrett's jaw and stomach   thousands

of lovely perfect sun balls
breaking at each other click
click click click like Saturday morning pistol cleaning
when the bullets hop across the bed sheet and bounce and click

click and you toss them across the floor like . . . up in the air
and see how many you can catch in one hand the left

oranges reeling across the room AND I KNOW I KNOW
it is my brain coming out like red grass
this breaking where red things wade

# DATES

It becomes apparent that I miss great occasions.
My birth was heralded by nothing
but the anniversary of Winston Churchill's marriage.
No monuments bled, no instruments
agreed on a specific weather.
It was a seasonal insignificance.

I console myself with my mother's eighth month.
While she sweated out her pregnancy in Ceylon
a servant ambling over the lawn
with a tray of iced drinks,
a few friends visiting her
to placate her shape, and I
drinking the life lines,
Wallace Stevens sat down in Connecticut
a glass of orange juice at his table
so hot he wore only shorts
and on the back of a letter
began to write 'The Well Dressed Man with a Beard'.

That night while my mother slept
her significant belly cooled
by the bedroom fan
Stevens put words together
that grew to sentences
and shaved them clean and
shaped them, the page suddenly
becoming thought where nothing had been,
his head making his hand
move where he wanted
and he saw his hand was saying
the mind is never finished, no, never
and I in my mother's stomach was growing
as were the flowers outside the Connecticut windows.

## WHITE DWARFS

This is for people who disappear
for those who descend into the code
and make their room a fridge for Superman
– who exhaust costume and bones that could perform flight,
who shave their moral so raw
they can tear themselves through the eye of a needle
this is for those people
that hover and hover
and die in the ether peripheries

There is my fear
of no words    of
falling without words
over and over    of
mouthing the silence
Why do I love most
among my heroes those
who sail to that perfect edge
where there is no social fuel
Release of sandbags
to understand their altitude –

        that silence of the third cross
        3rd man hung so high and lonely
        we don't hear him say
        say his pain, say his unbrotherhood
        What has he to do with the smell of ladies
        can they eat off his skeleton of pain?

The Gurkhas in Malaya
cut the tongues of mules
so they were silent beasts of burden
in enemy territories
after such cruelty what could they speak of anyway
And Dashiell Hammett in success
suffered conversation and moved
to the perfect white between the words

This white that can grow
is fridge, bed,
is an egg – most beautiful
when unbroken, where
what we cannot see is growing
in all the colours we cannot see

there are those burned out stars
who implode into silence
after parading in the sky
after such choreography what would they wish to speak of   anyway

**LIGHT**
*For Doris Gratiaen*


Midnight storm. Trees walking off across the fields in fury
naked in the spark of lightning.
I sit on the white porch on the brown hanging cane chair
coffee in my hand midnight storm midsummer night.
The past, friends and family, drift into the rain shower.
Those relatives in my favourite slides
re-shot from old minute photographs so they now stand
complex ambiguous grainy on my wall.

This is my Uncle who turned up to his marriage
on an elephant. He was a chaplain.
This shy looking man in the light jacket and tie was infamous,
when he went drinking he took the long blonde beautiful hair
of his wife and put one end in the cupboard and locked it
leaving her tethered in an armchair.
He was terrified of her possible adultery
and this way died peaceful happy to the end.
My Grandmother, who went to a dance in a muslin dress
with fireflies captured and embedded in the cloth, shining
and witty. This calm beautiful face
organized wild acts in the tropics.
She hid the mailman in her house
after he had committed murder and at the trial
was thrown out of the court for making jokes at the judge.
Her son became a Q.C.
This is my brother at 6. With his cousin and his sister
and Pam de Voss who fell on a penknife and lost her eye.
My Aunt Christie. She knew Harold Macmillan was a spy
communicating with him through pictures in the newspapers.
Every picture she believed asked her to forgive him, his hound eyes
    pleading.
Her husband Uncle Fitzroy a doctor in Ceylon had a mind and memory
sharp as scalpels in his 80's, though I never bothered to ask him
about anything – interested then more in the latest recordings of Bobby
    Darin.

And this is my Mother with her brother Noel in fancy dress.
They are 7 and 8 years old, a handcoloured photograph,
it is the earliest picture I have. It is the one I love most.
A picture of my kids at Halloween
has the same contact and the same laughter.
My Uncle dying at 68, and my Mother a year later dying at 68.
She told me about his death and the day he died
his eyes clearing out of his illness as if seeing
right through the room the hospital and she said
he saw something so clear and good that his whole body
for that moment became youthful and she remembered
when she sewed badges on his trackshirts.
Her voice joyous in telling me this, and her face light and clear.
(My firefly Grandmother also dying at 68.)

These are the fragments I have of them all, in my mind
tonight with my coffee in this storm, the dogs restless on the porch.
They were all laughing, crazy, and vivid in their prime.
At a party my drunk Father
tried to explain a complex operation on chickens
and managed to kill them all in the process, the guests
having dinner an hour later while my Father slept
and the kids watched the servants clean up the litter
of beaks and feathers on the lawn.

These are their fragments, all I remember of them,
wanting more knowledge of them. In the mirror and in my kids
I see them in my flesh. Wherever we are
they parade in my brain and the expanding stories
connect to the grey grainy pictures on the wall, as they hold their drinks
or 20 years later hold grandchildren, pose with favourite dogs,
coming through the light the electricity which the storm destroyed
an hour ago, a tree going down by the highway
so that now inside the kids play dominoes in candlelight
and out here the thick rain static the spark of my match to the cigarette
and the trees across the fields leaving me, distinct
lonely in their own knife scars and cow chewed bark
frozen in the jagged light as if snapped in their run
the branch arms waving to what was a second ago the dark sky
when in truth like me they haven't moved.
Haven't moved an inch from me.

# P. K. PAGE

## PRESENTATION

Now most miraculously the most junior clerk
becomes a hero.
Oh, beautiful child
projected suddenly to executive grandeur,
gone up like an angel in the air of good wishes,
the gift and the speeches.

Dry as chalk from your files you come, unfolding.
In the hothouse they have made of their hearts
you flower
and by a double magic, force their flower –
the gift repaid in the symbol of desire.
You have become quite simply glorious.
They by comparison cannot be less.

Oh, lighted by this dream, the office glows
brightly among the double row of desks.
This day shines in their breasts like emeralds,
their faces wake from sleeping as you smile.
They have achieved new grace because you leave.
Each, at this moment, has a home, has love.

# THE LANDLADY

Through sepia air the boarders come and go,
impersonal as trains. Pass silently
the craving silence swallowing her speech;
click doors like shutters on her camera eye.

Because of her their lives become exact:
their entrances and exits are designed;
phone calls are cryptic. Oh, her ticklish ears
advance and fall back stunned.

Nothing is unprepared. They hold the walls
about them as they weep or laugh. Each face
is dialled to zero publicly. She peers
stippled with curious flesh;

pads on the patient landing like a pulse,
unlocks their keyholes with the wire of sight,
searches their rooms for clues when they are out,
pricks when they come home late.

Wonders when they are quiet, jumps when they move,
dreams that they dope or drink, trembles to know
the traffic of their brains, jaywalks their street
in clumsy shoes.

Yet knows them better than their closest friends:
their cupboards and the secrets of their drawers,
their books, their private mail, their photographs
are theirs and hers.

Knows when they wash, how frequently their clothes
go to the cleaners, what they like to eat,
their curvature of health, but even so
is not content.

And like a lover must know all, all, all.
Prays she may catch them unprepared at last
and palm the dreadful riddle of their skulls –
hoping the worst.

## LITTLE GIRLS

More than discovery – rediscovery.
They renew
acquaintanceship with all things
as with flowers in dreams.

And delicate as a sketch made by being,
they merge in a singular way with their own thoughts,
drawing an arabesque with a spoon or fork
casually on the air behind their shoulders,
or talk in a confidential tone as if
their own ears held the hearing of another.

Legs in the dance go up as though on strings
pulled by their indifferent wanton hands

while anger blows into them and through their muslin
easily as sand or wind.

Older, they become round and hard, demand
shapes that are real, castles on the shore
and all the lines and angles of tradition
are mustered for them in their eagerness
to become whole, fit themselves to the thing
they see outside them,
while the thing they left
lies like a caul in some abandoned place,
unremembered by fingers or the incredibly bright
stones, which for a time replace their eyes.

## THE KNITTERS
*(for Alice and Sheila)*


These women knitting knit a kind of mist –
climate of labyrinth –
into the air.
Sitting like sleepers,
propped against the chintz,
pin-headed somehow – figures by Moore –
arachnes in their webs, they barely stir –

except their eyes and hands, which wired to some
urgent personal circuit,
move as if
a switch controlled them.
Hear the click and hum
as their machines translating hieroglyphs,
compulsive and monotonous, consume –
lozenge and hank – the candy-coloured stuff.

See two observe the ceremony of skeins:
one, forearms raised,
the loops around her palms,
catscradle rocks, is metronome, becalmed;
while her companion
spun from her as from
a wooden spindle, winds a woollen world.

A man rings like an axe, is alien,
imperilled by them,
finds them cold and far.
They count their stitches on a female star
and speak another language,
are not kin.
Or is he Theseus remembering
that maze, those daedal ways, the Minotaur?

They knit him out, the wool grows thick and fills
the room they sit in like a fur
as vegetable more than animal,
surrealist and slightly sinister,
driven by motors strong beyond their wills,
these milky plants devour
more hanks of wool, more cubic feet of air.


## MAN WITH ONE SMALL HAND


One hand is smaller than the other. It
must always be loved a little like a child;
requires attention constantly, implies
it needs his frequent glance to nurture it.

He holds it sometimes with the larger one
as adults lead a child across the street.
Finding it his or suddenly alien
rallies his interest and his sympathy.

Sometimes you come upon him unawares
just quietly staring at it where it lies
as mute and somehow perfect as a flower.

But no. It is not perfect. He admits
it has its faults: it is not strong or quick.
At night it vanishes to reappear
in dreams full-size, lost or surrealist.

Yet has its place like memory or a dog –
is never completely out of mind – a rod
to measure all uncertainties against.

Perhaps he loves it too much, sets too much stock
simply in its existence. Ah, but look!
It has its magic. See how it will fit
so sweetly, sweetly in the infant's glove.

# MINERAL

Soft and unmuscular among the flowers and papers
and changed as if grown deaf or slightly lame
she writes to strangers about him as if he were a stranger,
avoids the name
which he no longer has a use for, which
he disinherited as he was leaving.
It had a different ring when he was living.

Now he is mineral to her. In a game
she would declare him mineral without thinking.
Mineral his going and his having gone
and on her desk, his photo – mineral.

No gentle mirage loves her as a dream
can love a person's head, no memory
comes warm and willing to her tears. She walks
nearly begonia between the walls,
calls out against an echo. Nothing's real
but mineral: cold touch, sharp taste of it
lodger forever in her routed house.

## PHOTOS OF A SALT MINE

How innocent their lives look,
how like a child's
dream of caves and winter, both combined;
the steep descent to whiteness
and the stope
with its striated walls
their folds all leaning as if pointing to
the greater whiteness still,
that great white bank
with its decisive front,
that seam upon a slope,
salt's lovely ice.

And wonderful underfoot the snow of salt
the fine
particles a broom could sweep,
one thinks
muckers might make angels in its drifts
as children do in snow,
lovers in sheets,
lie down and leave imprinted where they lay
a feathered creature holier than they.

And in the outworked stopes
with lamps and ropes
up miniature matterhorns
the miners climb
probe with their lights
the ancient folds of rock –
syncline and anticline –
and scoop from darkness an Aladdin's cave:
rubies and opals glitter from its walls.

But hoses douse the brilliance of these jewels,
melt fire to brine.
Salt's bitter water trickles thin and forms,
slow fathoms down,
a lake within a cave,
lacquered with jet –
white's opposite.
There grey on black the boating miners float
to mend the stays and struts of that old stope
and deeply underground
their words resound,
are multiplied by echo, swell and grow
and make a climate of a miner's voice.

So all the photographs like children's wishes
are filled with caves or winter,
innocence
has acted as a filter,
selected only beauty from the mine.
Except in the last picture,
it is shot
from an acute high angle. In a pit
figures the size of pins are strangely lit
and might be dancing but you know they're not.
Like Dante's vision of the nether hell
men struggle with the bright cold fires of salt,
locked in the black inferno of the rock:
the filter here, not innocence but guilt.

## ELEMENT

Feeling my face has the terrible shine of fish
caught and swung on a line under the sun
I am frightened held in the light that people make
and sink in darkness freed and whole again
as fish returned by dream into the stream.

Oh running water is not rough; ruffled to eye,
to flesh it is flat and smooth; to fish
silken as children's hands in milk.

I am not wishful in this dream of immersion.
Mouth becomes full with darkness
and the shine, mottled and pastel, sounds its own note, not
the fake high treble thrown on resounding faces.

There are flowers – and this is pretty for the summer –
light on the bed of darkness;
there are stones that glisten and grow slime;
winters that question nothing, are a new
night for the passing movement of fine fins;
and quietly, by the reeds or water fronds
something can cry without discovery.

Ah in daylight the shine is single
as dime flipped or gull on fire or fish
silently hurt – its mouth alive with metal.

# THE PERMANENT TOURISTS

Somnolent through landscapes and by trees
nondescript, almost anonymous,
they alter as they enter foreign cities –
the terrible tourists with their empty eyes
longing to be filled with monuments.

Verge upon statues in the public squares
remembering the promise of memorials
yet never enter the entire event
as dogs, abroad in any kind of weather,
move perfectly within their rainy climate.

Lock themselves into snapshots on the steps
of monolithic bronze as if suspecting
the subtle mourning of the photograph
might later conjure in the memory
all they are now incapable of feeling.

And search all heroes out: the boy who gave
his life to save a town; the stolid queen;
forgotten politicians minus names
and the plunging war dead, permanently brave,
forever and ever going down to death.

Look, you can see them nude in any café
reading their histories from the bill of fare,
creating futures from a foreign teacup.
Philosophies like ferns bloom from the fable
that travel is broadening at the café table.

Yet somehow beautiful, they stamp the plaza.
Classic in their anxiety they call
all sculptured immemorial stone
into their passive eyes, as rivers
draw ruined columns to their placid glass.

# THEY MIGHT HAVE BEEN ZEBRAS
*(for Margaret)*


They might have been zebras. I'd have been no more surprised
than to see by daylight four night raccoons, full-grown
walking bear-like in indian file across
our isthmus of bright grass
so black and white, their fur so fluffed and upright
black masked, tails ringed with black and white
utterly foreign to morning's minted light
and violent as newsprint on the viridian lawn.

It's not that they're unfamiliar. We have met
dozens of times in darkness. They've climbed and gazed
down at me from the Douglas fir's right-angled boughs –
sly and furtive watchers – or, bold and wild
hauled from our obsidian pool gold fish whose scales
in the moonlight shine like pieces of eight.
We acknowledge each other at night. We meet and stare
shadowy form at shadowy form. I chain the dog
leave offerings for them of marshmallows, raisins, bread.

But by day they immobilize me. I hold my breath.
Turn to a great soft statue with inflammable eyes
tinder for the fire they strike from the morning air.
And I see them blacker and whiter than I had dreamed
sharper, more feral, spanning the grassy isthmus
as if there might be others in front and behind –
a whole parade extending to both horizons
but hidden by the berried cotoneasters.

When they disappear I am released.
Dart through the door.
The sun is sharpening every leaf.
Its threads are spinning a golden tent.
The green is enamel or emeralds.
Petals fall more fragile than flakes of snow.
I alone, unbeautiful, in the whole morning
in flapping nightdress search every bush.
But the four who blinded me are gone.
Is this grey ash all that is left?

## THE MURDER

Trying to put an end to what is endless
trying to terminate what is outside time
is to be set upon a fruitless murder.

That body cannot die. Instead
and many years later one bright day
I found myself – dismembered, foul

in a small box. Legs, torso, arms.

Who butchered the body and put it there?
Who buried these bones, this brittle hair?

Heart – black, shrivelled – a pullet's heart.

Let air and sunlight miracle
the loathesome contents. Let the grey
bones whiten and sort themselves and beg

forgiveness for their attempted murder
of a body existing outside time
and indestructible, being endless.

# AL PURDY

## THE CARIBOO HORSES

At 100 Mile House the cowboys ride in rolling
stagey cigarettes with one hand reining
half-tame bronco rebels on a morning grey as stone
– so much like riding dangerous women
          with whiskey coloured eyes –
such women as once fell dead with their lovers
with fire in their heads and slippery froth on thighs
– Beaver or Carrier women maybe or
          Blackfoot squaws far past the edge of this valley
on the other side of those two toy mountain ranges
          from the sunfierce plains beyond

But only horses
                    waiting in stables
hitched at taverns
                    standing at dawn
pastured outside the town with
jeeps and fords and chevvys and
busy muttering stake trucks rushing
importantly over roads of man's devising
over the safe known roads of the ranchers
families and merchants of the town
                    On the high prairie
are only horse and rider
                    wind in dry grass
clopping in silence under the toy mountains
dropping sometimes and
                    lost in the dry grass
                    golden oranges of dung

Only horses
        no stopwatch memories or palace ancestors
not Kiangs hauling undressed stone in the Nile Valley
and having stubborn Egyptian tantrums or
Onagers racing thru Hither Asia and
the last Quagga screaming in African highlands
              lost relatives of these
              whose hooves were thunder
the ghosts of horses battering thru the wind
whose names were the wind's common usage
whose life was the sun's
              arriving here at chilly noon
              in the gasoline smell of the
              dust and waiting 15 minutes
              at the grocer's


**PERCY LAWSON**
*(Contract Negotiator - Vancouver Upholsterers' Union)*


Sitting with Lawson in 1954
        sitting with Percy Lawson
ill at ease in the boss's panelled office
after work hours talking of nothing
talking of practically almost nothing
a lousy nickel raise that is
        haggling over a lousy nickel
and maybe besides the long and hourly
bearable toil of an almost lifetime
(East Indians: 35 years
        Canadians: 70 – figures approximate)
Listen in again in the boss's panelled office
        listen to Lawson
listen to Percy Lawson
– thinking of girls in the cutting room
afraid of the union
        afraid for their jobs and
thinking of me – afraid of Watt or
not afraid

only wanting to be liked
and knowing for sure I'm not
Thinking of Lawson
         up from the coal mines
on the island and gotten fat
since talking and haggling and
being afraid of practically nothing
but death and his wife and damn near
         everything but not
bosses
not Watt
And what's the contract news from Watt who
if I said what I thought he was would
sue me for damn near everything
would sue me right now in a poem and
get a judgment for one lying lyric
         I can't write
         (I'll be damned if I write)
in praise of Watt
in praise of
         practically nothing
But I listen to Percy Lawson
         haggling over a lousy nickel
listen to the sonuvabitch
         haggling over a lousy nickel
the twentieth part of a dollar that
         winks among the words
like a clean magician's coin
born from virginal nothing and not
mined or smelted and sweated and laboured for for
the twentieth part of a wasted hour back there
in the silvery guts of a labouring terribly useful lifetime
In a tactical pause between the chop
         of words Lawson turns
the little fat man probably dead now
         turns then
and gives me a gold-toothed grin.

## ARCTIC RHODODENDRONS

They are small purple surprises
in the river's white racket
and after you've seen them
a number of times
in water-places
where their silence seems
related to river-thunder
you think of them as 'noisy flowers'
Years ago
it may have been
that lovers came this way
stopped in the outdoor hotel
to watch the water floorshow
and lying prone together
where the purged green
boils to a white heart
and the shore trembles
like a stone song
flowers were their conversation
and love the sound of a colour
that lasts two weeks in August
and then dies
except for the three or four
I pressed in a letter
and sent whispering to you.

*Pangnirtung*

## POEM

You are ill and so I lead you away
and put you to bed in the dark room
– you lie breathing softly and I hold your hand
feeling the fingertips relax as sleep comes

You will not sleep more than a few hours
and the illness is less serious than my anger or cruelty
and the dark bedroom is like a foretaste of other darknesses
to come later which all of us must endure alone
but here I am permitted to be with you

After a while in sleep your fingers clutch tightly
and I know that whatever may be happening
the fear coiled in dreams or the bright trespass of pain
there is nothing at all I can do except hold your hand
and not go away

## POEM FOR ONE OF THE ANNETTES

Which one of you? – oh now
I recognize that tear-strained pro-
Semitic nose shaped wonderfully for
your man Murray's kisses but
he left didn't he?
    Oh Annette
                cry like hell
for Columbus Ohio and Taos New Mexico
where he is and you're not
                      As if
the world had ended and
            it has –

Or the Anita with undressed hips that
could break a man in half in bed and
big unpainted Rubens breasts affixed to
           a living woman
swinging high over Montreal
                   As if
the whole damn town was a whorehouse full
of literarily inclined millionaires with a yen
for your kind of dirty-story-book-love and
           it is –

Or Janine from Poland who's
a citizen of Canada knocked up
in Montreal by a Yank from
Columbus Ohio and
           abandoned and
the abortion took place in the Town of
Mount Royal and the foetus had
           no name –

Cry for your own bad judgment in
  loving him with good tears that
    will not
          fall
        but stay
in the blue beginning of every evening when
factory watchmen are coming on duty and
silent lovers are visible as moths hovering on
streetcorners
          in eccentric silver orbit
as permanent as any in
          Maisonneuve's cynical metropolis –

Cry the common sickness with ordinary tears
                    As if
they would flood the whole quasi-romantic town of
Montreal with the light of your darkness and
follow the gutters and sewers glowing down
thru sewage disposal plants by the river and
into the industrial waste of your dreams to
        the sea
          the shapeless mothering one-celled sea –

Oh Anita, they do.

## ROBLIN'S MILLS (2)


The wheels stopped
and the murmur of voices
behind the flume's tremble
stopped
            and the wind-high ships
that sailed from Rednersville
to the sunrise ports of Europe
are delayed somewhere
in a toddling breeze
The black millpond
turns an unreflecting eye
to look inward
like an idiot child
locked in the basement
when strangers come
whizzing past on the highway
above the dark green valley
a hundred yards below
The mill space is empty
even stones are gone
where hands were shaken
and walls enclosed laughter
saved up and brought here
from the hot fields
where all stories
are rolled into one
And white dust floating
above the watery mumble
and bright human sounds
to shimmer among the pollen
where bees dance now
Of all these things
no outline remains
no shadow on the soft air
no bent place in the heat glimmer
where the heavy walls pressed

And some of those who vanished
lost children of the time
kept after school
left alone in a graveyard
who may not change
or ever grow six inches
in one hot summer
or turn where the great herons
graze the sky's low silver
– stand between the hours
in a rotting village
near the weed-grown eye
that looks into itself
deep in the black crystal
that holds and contains
the substance of shadows
manner and custom
  of the inarticulate
departures and morning rumours
gestures and almost touchings
announcements and arrivals
gossip of someone's marriage
when a girl or tired farm woman
whose body suddenly blushes
beneath a faded house dress
with white expressionless face
turns to her awkward husband
to remind him of something else
The black millpond
    holds them
movings and reachings and fragments
the gear and tackle of living
under the water eye
all things laid aside
    discarded
    forgotten
but they had their being once
and left a place to stand on

# THE COUNTRY NORTH OF BELLEVILLE

Bush land scrub land –
    Cashel Township and Wollaston
Elzevir McClure and Dungannon
green lands of Weslemkoon Lake
where a man might have some
    opinion of what beauty
is and none deny him
          for miles –

Yet this is the country of defeat
where Sisyphus rolls a big stone
year after year up the ancient hills
picnicking glaciers have left strewn
with centuries' rubble
         backbreaking days
         in the sun and rain
when realization seeps slow in the mind
without grandeur or self deception in
         noble struggle
of being a fool –

A country of quiescence and still distance
a lean land
     not like the fat south
with inches of black soil on
     earth's round belly –
And where the farms are
     it's as if a man stuck
both thumbs in the stony earth and pulled

                    it apart
                    to make room
enough between the trees
for a wife
             and maybe some cows and
             room for some
of the more easily kept illusions –
And where the farms have gone back
to forest
             are only soft outlines
             shadowy differences –
Old fences drift vaguely among the trees
             a pile of moss-covered stones
gathered for some ghost purpose
has lost meaning under the meaningless sky
             – they are like cities under water
and the undulating green waves of time
             are laid on them –

This is the country of our defeat
             and yet
during the fall plowing a man
might stop and stand in a brown valley of the furrows
             and shade his eyes to watch for the same
             red patch mixed with gold
             that appears on the same
             spot in the hills
             year after year
             and grow old
plowing and plowing a ten-acre field until
the convolutions run parallel with his own brain –

And this is a country where the young
                    leave quickly
unwilling to know what their fathers know
or think the words their mothers do not say –

Herschel Monteagle and Faraday
lakeland rockland and hill country
a little adjacent to where the world is
a little north of where the cities are and
sometime
we may go back there
                    to the country of our defeat
Wollaston Elzevir and Dungannon
and Weslemkoon lake land
where the high townships of Cashel
                    McClure and Marmora once were –
But it's been a long time since
and we must enquire the way
          of strangers –

## DEPRESSION IN NAMU, B.C.


The eagle's passage sings there
crossing the sky on a high wire
salmon leap to find their other selves
black bear amble to breakfast at the river
the sun floats thru a blue notch in the hills

There was never a time
I did not know about such a place
to match the imagined place in my mind
– but I have lived too long somewhere else
and beauty bores me without the slight ache
of ugliness that makes me want to change things
knowing it's impossible

## TOURIST ITINERARY

North of Kirkland Lake raspberries are red earrings
in heat like a tropic summer
but even in August nights are cold
trees shrink a little past the height of land
that slopes down the arctic watershed
Driving north
a bear crosses the road
at his private pedestrian crossing
the first animal we had seen
and almost asked for his autograph
Then Cochrane and the train to Moosonee
over the soft spongy trapper's country
crossing and re-crossing the Abitibi
until it joins the big Moose
our elderly train jogging the river valley
past rocks like the heads of queens
Indians with closed faces at Moose Factory
huge wood piles and shabby houses
selling bannock and toy boats for a living
knowing it isn't a very good one
know it's the best there is
I add another piece of mosaic
to the coloured memory inside
I know what the place looks like
tasted the food and touched the land
which is as much as any of us can do
following a road map in the mind
a memory of the place we came from
and the way we are always returning

# JAMES REANEY

## MRS. WENTWORTH

I was tired of evenings of euchre
Of waltzing and dancing with fools.
There was nothing to look at in the sky.
The moon had disappeared
And the stars bore me.

Ink gleams wet only a moment
After a person writes.
So I gleamed only a moment
After eighteen years with a Wentworth.
Now Mr. Wentworth was a prominent practitioner
Of one of the religions of this city.

I was sick of reading Spurgeon
I was tired of singing Moody
I was positive I wouldn't burgeon
In the Congregational Choir.
And I thought I once had been saved
Ship Ahoy
And I once had been laved
In the precious blood of the Lamb
Ship Ahoy and Rescue the perishing.
It was then I decided
That I
Would have looked rather silly
On a cross.

Then I took to taking walks in the country
Just at the edge of town
(The houses like runs in rummy.)
With a certain Mr. O'Flaherty.
We smelt the fields of buckwheat together.
In those days I had a lump
On the white back of my neck
And he sang to me

That when I would kiss him real hard
He'd give me a handkerchief
For my inside coat-pocket
And a handkerchief for my outside coat-pocket
And he said he knew some liniment
To take my lump away.

But he gave me a swelling in front
And now I fear the Lord.
Oh give me a grenade against him
I cannot stand his toasted smile
And his red hair.
And oh what shall I do
When the roll is called up yonder?
There is nothing to look at in the sky
The moon has disappeared
And the stars bore me.

*1947*

# THE RED HEART

The only leaf upon its tree of blood,
My red heart hangs heavily
And will never fall loose,
But grow so heavy
After only a certain number of seasons
(Sixty winters, and fifty-nine falls,
Fifty-eight summers, and fifty-seven springs)
That it will bring bough
Tree and the fences of my bones
Down to a grave in the forest
Of my still upright fellows.

So does the sun hang now
From a branch of Time
In this wild fall sunset.
Who shall pick the sun
From the tree of Eternity?
Who shall thresh the ripe sun?
What midwife shall deliver
The Sun's great heir?
It seems that no one can,
And so the sun shall drag
Gods, goddesses and parliament buildings,
Time, Fate, gramaphones and Man
To a gray grave
Where all shall be trampled
Beneath the dancing feet of crowds
Of other still-living suns and stars.

## THE ROYAL VISIT

When the King and the Queen came to Stratford
Everyone felt at once
How heavy the Crown must be.
The Mayor shook hands with their Majesties
And everyone presentable was presented
And those who weren't have resented
It, and will
To their dying day.
Everyone had almost a religious experience
When the King and Queen came to visit us
(I wonder what they felt!)
And hydrants flowed water in the gutters
All day.
People put quarters on the railroad tracks
So as to get squashed by the Royal Train
And some people up the line at Shakespeare
Stayed in Shakespeare, just in case –
They did stop too,
While thousands in Stratford
Didn't even see them
Because the Engineer didn't slow down
Enough in time.
And although,
But although we didn't see them in any way
(I didn't even catch the glimpse
The teacher who was taller did
Of a gracious pink figure)
I'll remember it to my dying day.

# THE UPPER CANADIAN

I wish I had been born beside a river
Instead of this round pond
Where the geese white as pillows float
In continual circles
And never get out.

Sometimes I wish that I
Hadn't been born in this dull township
Where fashion, thought and wit
Never penetrate,
Unless the odd quotation from Handy Andy
Is really what I demand,
What I want.

The river, the railroad,
And His Majesty's Highways
Number Seven and Eight
Go through town
And never are the same again.
But this pond and I
Go through and become
Nothing different.
Now if I went away
And left this little lake,
If I struck out for the railroad and the river,
I might lose my way.
I would have to win a scholarship
Or build a Punch and Judy Show.
I'd better not,
I'd better stay.
And watch the darning-needle flies
Fly and glitter in the shining wind
Of summer by this pond.

At night I'll read
*The Collected Works of William Shakespeare*
By an empty stove
And think at least there's this
Although I'll never see it acted.
I'll hear the rain outside
And, if it's August,
A cricket's sharp chirp in the pantry.
I won't go away
Unless it rains and rains
Making the pond so large
That it joins the river,
But it never will.
I shall always sit here in this hovel
Weeping perhaps over an old Victorian novel
And hear the dingy interwinding tunes
Of country rain and wind
And lame fires of damp wood.
Especially shall I hear that starved cricket
My mind, that thinks a railway ticket
Could save it from its enclosed, cramped quality.
That mind where thoughts float round
As geese do round a pond
And never get out.

## THE KATZENJAMMER KIDS

With porcupine locks
And faces which, when
More closely examined,
Are composed of measle-pink specks,
These two dwarf imps,
The Katzenjammer Kids,
Flitter through their Desert Island world.
Sometimes they get so out of hand
That a blue Captain
With stiff whiskers of black wicker
And an orange Inspector
With a black telescope
Pursue them to spank them
All through that land
Where cannibals cut out of brown paper
In cardboard jungles feast and caper,
Where the sea's sharp waves continually
Waver against the shore faithfully
And the yellow sun above is thin and flat
With a collar of black spikes and spines
To tell the innocent childish heart that
It shines
And warms (see where she stands and stammers)
The dear fat mother of the Katzenjammers.
Oh, for years and years she has stood
At the window and kept fairly good
Guard over the fat pies that she bakes
For her two children, those dancing heartaches.
Oh, the blue skies of that funny paper weather!
The distant birds like two eyebrows close together!
And the rustling paper roar
Of the waves
Against the paper sands of the paper shore!

# THE HUMMINGBIRD

The hum of an approaching christening mob!
The hanging still in the air with so much motion
He flies with wings of air in an air of feathers!
The hanging still in the air with so much motion

The hollow twig that transports flowers to his blood
The barn of flowers pressed in a jumping ounce
No song is needed when one is a song
The barn of flowers pressed in a jumping ounce

Enoch, Elijah or Ascension is your name
My dainty jaunt, why call I you these names?
Because I realize and advertise that there
Far down the dark row of mountains cowering
That ruby flash that is the chariot of fire
                    Is your throat too.

*1958*

# THE MORNING DEW

Shake seed of light and thunder
From where you hang,
The Word without the Flesh.

The pastures, sloughs and trees all shine
Their leaves and grasses sown
With flashing tears.

Here is Absalom's hair in crystal terms
Feverish bonfire of the sensual body,
Bloodbob.

Sharp, sharp yellow teeth, sharp sharp
In the dark mouth blinking of the
Fox-haired queen.

Blue as the fields of flax in the summer
That dream of retting, spreading, drying,
White linen snow.

Green as the thoughtful ancient woods
Ash contemplation of linden tree thinking,
Paththrough.

The killdeer's nest is built of gold,
Cobwebs are blessed and Eden
Has caught these fields within her fold.

*1958*

## FIRST LETTER
### *To the Avon River above Stratford, Canada*

What did the Indians call you?
For you do not flow
With English accents.
I hardly know
What I should call you
    Because before
I drank coffee or tea
    I drank you
    With my cupped hands
And you did not taste English to me
    And you do not sound
    Like Avon
    Or swans & bards
But rather like the sad wild fowl
    In prints drawn
    By Audubon
And like dear bad poets
    Who wrote
    Early in Canada
And never were of note.
You are the first river
    I crossed
And like the first whirlwind
    The first rainbow
    First snow, first
    Falling star I saw,
You, for other rivers are my law.
    These other rivers:
    The Red & the Thames
    Are never so sweet
To skate upon, swim in
    Or for baptism of sin.

Silver and light
The sentence of your voice,
        With a soprano
Continuous cry you shall
        Always flow
        Through my heart.
The rain and the snow of my mind
Shall supply the spring of that river
        Forever.
Though not your name
Your coat of arms I know
        And motto:
A shield of reeds and cresses
        Sedges, crayfishes
The hermaphroditic leech
Minnows, muskrats and farmers' geese
And printed above this shield
One of my earliest wishes
"To flow like you."

## SIXTH LETTER
*A House on King William Street*


Like the life here
The wallpaper repeats itself
Up and down go the roses
Similar blows struck out
By air-banging green fists:
A bright rose and a blue one
A pink blow and a blue one

The years have not changed their likeness
Except that those behind the sofa
Have kept their original blaze
And these opposite the window
Have turned yellow.

Aunt Henny says to Aunt Penny,
"Have you read *She?* Oh a terrible book,
An awful book! Yes, it's by
Haggard Rider Haggard."

Aunt Lurkey says to Aunt Turkey:
"I nearly slipped today, I nearly
Slipped today.
We should put a piece of carpet
On that particular step
We should,"
Says Aunt Lurkey taking another should
Off the would pile.

No one remembers when
The wallpaper was new, except
The wallpaper itself
In the green smothered darkness behind
The sofa and the cupboard.

And I, I their awkward fool
Board there while I go to school.

# F. R. SCOTT

## TRANS CANADA

Pulled from our ruts by the made-to-order gale
We sprang upward into a wider prairie
And dropped Regina below like a pile of bones.

Sky tumbled upon us in waterfalls,
But we were smarter than a Skeena salmon
And shot our silver body over the lip of air
To rest in a pool of space
On the top storey of our adventure.

A solar peace
And a six-way choice.

Clouds, now, are the solid substance,
A floor of wool roughed by the wind
Standing in waves that halt in their fall.
A still of troughs.

The plane, our planet,
Travels on roads that are not seen or laid
But sound in instruments on pilots' ears,

While underneath
The sure wings
Are the everlasting arms of science.

Man, the lofty worm, tunnels his latest clay,
And bores his new career.

This frontier, too, is ours.
This everywhere whose life can only be led
At the pace of a rocket
Is common to man and man,
And every country below is an I land.

The sun sets on its top shelf,
And stars seem farther from our nearer grasp.

I have sat by night beside a cold lake
And touched things smoother than moonlight on still water,
But the moon on this cloud sea is not human,
And here is no shore, no intimacy,
Only the start of space, the road to suns.

## TO CERTAIN FRIENDS

I see my friends now standing about me, bemused,
Eyeing me dubiously as I pursue my course,
Clutching their little less that is world's away.

Full of good will, they greet me with offers of help,
Now and then with the five-dollar-bill of evasion,
Sincere in their insincerity; believing, in unbelief.

The nation's needs are to them considerable problems.
Often they play no bridge nor sit at the movies,
Preferring to hear some expert discuss every angle.

They show great zeal collecting the news and statistics.
They know far more about every question than I do,
But their knowledge of how to use knowledge grows
        smaller and smaller.

They make a virtue of having an open mind,
Open to endless arrivals of other men's suggestions,
To the rain of facts that deepens the drought of the will.

Above all they fear the positive formation of opinion,
The essential choice that acts as a mental compass,
The clear perception of the road to the receding horizon.

For this would mean leaving the shade of the middle ground
To walk in the open air, and in unknown places;
Might lead, perhaps – dread thought! – to definite action.

They will grow old seeking to avoid conclusions,
Refusing to learn by living, to test by trying,
Letting opportunities slip from their tentative fingers,

Till one day, after the world has tired of waiting,
While they are busy arguing about the obvious,
A half-witted demagogue will walk away with their children.

# A GRAIN OF RICE

Such majestic rhythms, such tiny disturbances.
The rain of the monsoon falls, an inescapable treasure,
Hundreds of millions live
Only because of the certainty of this season,
    The turn of the wind.

The frame of our human house rests on the motion
Of earth and of moon, the rise of continents,
Invasion of deserts, erosion of hills,
    The capping of ice.

Today, while Europe tilted, drying the Baltic,
I read of a battle between brothers in anguish,
    A flag moved a mile.

And today, from a curled leaf cocoon, in the course of its rhythm,
I saw the break of a shell, the creation
Of a great Asian moth, radiant, fragile,
Incapable of not being born, and trembling
    To live its brief moment.

Religions build walls round our love, and science
Is equal of error and truth. Yet always we find
Such ordered purpose in cell and in galaxy,
So great a glory in life-thrust and mind-range,
Such widening frontiers to draw out our longings,
    We grow to one world
    Through enlargement of wonder.

## ON SAYING GOOD-BYE TO MY ROOM
## IN CHANCELLOR DAY HALL

Rude and rough men are invading my sanctuary.
They are carting away all my books and papers.
My pictures are stacked in an ugly pile in the corner.
    There is murder in my cathedral.

The precious files, filled with yesterday's writing,
The letters from friends long dead, the irreplaceable evidence
Of battles now over, or worse, still in full combat –
    Where are they going? How shall I find them again?

Miserable vandals, stuffing me into your cartons,
This is a functioning office, all things are in order,
Or in that better disorder born of long usage.
    I alone can command it.

I alone know the secret thoughts in these cabinets,
And how the letters relate to the pamphlets in boxes.
I alone know the significance of underlinings
    On the pages read closely.

You scatter these sources abroad, and who then shall use them?
Oh, I am told, they will have a small place in some basement.
Gladly some alien shelves in a distant library
    Will give them safe shelter.

But will there be pictures of J. S. Woodsworth and Coldwell
Above the Supreme Court Reports? The Universal Declaration
Of Human Rights, will it be found hanging
    Near the left-wing manifestos?

And where are the corners to hold all the intimate objects
Gathered over the rich, the incredible years?
The sprig of cedar, the segment of Boulder Dam cable,
The heads of Buddha and Dante, the concretions, the arrow-heads,
    Where, where will they be?

Or the clock that was taken from my 1923 air-cooled Franklin?
The card-board Padlock, a gift from awakened students?
The Oxford oar, the Whitefield Quebec, the Lorcini?
    These cry out my history.

These are all cells to my brain, a part of my total.
Each filament thought feeds them into the process
By which we pursue the absolute truth that eludes us.
    They shared my decisions.

Now they are going, and I stand again on new frontiers.
Forgive this moment of weakness, this backward perspective.
Old baggage, I wish you good-bye and good housing.
    I strip for more climbing.

# DANCING

Long ago
when I first danced
I danced
holding her
back and arm
making her move
as I moved

she was best
when she was
least herself
lost herself

Now I dance
seeing her dance
away from me
                    she
looks at me
dancing
            we
are closer
held in the movement of the dance

I no longer dance
with myself

we are two
not one

the dance
is one

# MACKENZIE RIVER

This river belongs
  wholly to itself
    obeying its own laws

Its wide brown eye
  softens what it reflects
    from sky and shore

The top water   calm
  moves purposefully
    to a cold sea

Underneath   its stone bed
  shows sunken rock
    in swirl and surface wave

Suspended
  in its liquid force
    is the soil of deltas

The servient valleys
  reach up to lake and spring
    in clefts of far hills

And shed
  arteries of streams
    that stain the central flood

In spring thaw and spate
  its wide levels
    rise slowly   fall

Like tides
  that start upstream
  and die at sea

A river so Canadian
  it turns its back
  on America

The Arctic shore
  receives the vast flow
    a maze of ponds and dikes

In land so bleak and bare
  a single plume of smoke
    is a scroll of history.

# A. J. M. SMITH

## FIELD OF LONG GRASS

When she walks in the field of long grass
The delicate little hands of the grass
Lean forward a little to touch her.

Light is like the waving of the long grass.
Light is the faint to and fro of her dress.
Light rests for a while in her bosom.

When it is all gone from her bosom's hollow
And out of the field of long grass,
She walks in the dark by the edge of the fallow land.

Then she begins to walk in my heart.
Then she walks in me, swaying in my veins.

My wrists are a field of long grass
A little wind is kissing.

# THE SORCERER

There is a sorcerer in Lachine
Who for a small fee will put a spell
On my beloved, who has sea-green
Eyes, and on my doting self as well.

He will transform us, if we like, to goldfish:
We shall swim in a crystal bowl,
And the bright water will go swish
Over our naked bodies; we shall have no soul.

In the morning the syrupy sunshine
Will dance on our tails and fins.
I shall have her then all for mine,
And Father Lebeau will hear no more of her sins.

Come along, good sir, change us into goldfish.
I would put away intellect and lust,
Be but a red gleam in a crystal dish,
But kin of the trembling ocean, not of the dust.

# RESURRECTION OF ARP

On the third day rose Arp
out of the black sleeve of the tomb:
he could see like a cat in the dark,
but the light left him dumb.

He stood up to testify,
and his tongue wouldn't work
in the old groove; he had to try
other tongues, including the Scandinavian.

The saints were all well pleased;
his periods rattled and rolled;
heresies scattered like ninepins;
all the tickets were sold.

When they turned down the gas
everybody could see there was
a halo of tongues of pale fire
licking the grease off his hair,

and a white bird
fluttered away in the rafters;
people heard
the breaking of a mysterious wind (laughter).

He spoke another language
majestic beautiful wild
holy superlative believable
and undefiled

by any comprehensible
syllable
to provoke dissent
or found a schism . . . .

After the gratifyingly large
number of converts had been given receipts
the meeting adjourned to the social hall
for sexual intercourse (dancing) and eats.

Arp talked to the reporters:
on the whole, was glad to have cheated the tomb,
though the angels had been 'extremely courteous',
and death, after all, was only 'another room'.

## NEWS OF THE PHOENIX

They say the Phoenix is dying, some say dead.
Dead without issue is what one message said,
But that has been suppressed, officially denied.

I think myself the man who sent it lied.
In any case, I'm told, he has been shot,
As a precautionary measure, whether he did or not.

# FAR WEST

Among the cigarettes and the peppermint creams
Came the flowers of fingers, luxurious and bland,
Incredibly blossoming in the little breast.
And in the Far West
The tremendous cowboys in goatskin pants
Shot up the town of her ignorant wish.

In the gun flash she saw the long light shake
Across the lake, repeating that poem
At Finsbury Park.
But the echo was drowned in the roll of the trams –
Anyway, who would have heard? Not a soul.
Not one noble and toxic like Buffalo Bill.

In the holy name *bang! bang!* the flowers came
With the marvellous touch of fingers
Gentler than the fuzzy goats
Moving up and down up and down as if in ecstasy
As the cowboys rode their skintight stallions
Over the barbarous hills of California.

## THE WISDOM OF OLD JELLY ROLL

How all men wrongly death to dignify
Conspire, I tell. Parson, poetaster, pimp,
Each acts or acquiesces. They prettify,
Dress up, deodorize, embellish, primp,
And make a show of Nothing. Ah, but met-
aphysics laughs: she touches, tastes, and smells
– Hence knows – the diamond holes that make a net.
Silence resettled testifies to bells.
'Nothing' depends on 'Thing', which is or was:
So death makes life or makes life's worth, a worth
Beyond all highfalutin' woes or shows
To publish and confess. 'Cry at the birth,
Rejoice at the death,' old Jelly Roll said,
Being on whisky, ragtime, chicken, and the scriptures fed.

# RAYMOND SOUSTER

## JEANNETTE

Jeannette in a fight
calling in boy friends
to wreck a café,
Jeannette dead drunk
swinging at a cop,
Jeannette on the habit
riding it up
riding it down,
Jeannette in jail
and out again,
Jeannette on the corner
of Dundas and Jarvis
with the old reliable
merchandise for sale.

Some day they'll find her
with a knife in the chest,
or choked to death
by one sheer stocking:

but tonight she's the queen
of this crawling street,
Jeannette with her sweater tight,
proud to show them off
to all the boys:

black hair, big smile,
that's Jeannette.

## THE LAUNCHING

Any big event must have
the Ceremony of the Officials.

I had my officials picked out
long before starting to build
my master space rocket.
They included cabinet ministers,
arms makers, generals,
all the boys on the real inside.

When the Big Day came
they stood on a platform
at the foot of the monster
and made speeches
one after the other.

I let them talk
as long as they wanted to,
then, when the last one had finished,
I pushed back a little door
in the side of my brain-child
and invited them to enter.

When the last one had disappeared inside,
I closed the door, walked very deliberately
across to the control panel
and pushed a button.

Imagine my surprise
when it worked.

# EASTER SUNDAY

The day begins
too well. The wind
summer's, out
of season,
the sun, shy
behind clouds,
surely will burst through
in brilliance
soon.

But rain with thunder
before evening.
Behind the stone
rolled away
another and another
without end.

## ARMADALE AVENUE REVISITED

Street of my boyhood
(I lived right around the corner),
quiet, leaf-heavy street
of West Toronto.
                    Here,
behind that house, in the lane,
from garage roofs we ambushed
the Nelles Street gang,
pinned them down with catapults,
then, out of acorns,
forgot all our strategy
and ran like hell.
                    Out this door
on Christmas Day
of all days, that queer girl
came sleep-walking, nightgown and all,
and even the snow underfoot
couldn't waken her.
                    At this number lived
the grease-monkey boys,
(their Stutz Touring shined
to a blinding dazzle),
who sometimes took me
as heart-pounding passenger
out the Queen Elizabeth,
to run her, gun her
past eighty on a straight stretch,
with the extra spice
of maybe a speed-cop
coming out of nowhere.
                    On this lawn
I pounded and bloodied
my next-to-worst enemy,
and curiously found
it wasn't fun anymore. . . .

But tonight it's only
ghosts I see around these houses,
the old gang gone,
every one of them;
some killed in war,
some from natural causes,
the rest, I can guess,
growing fat and middle-aged
like me.
            But not one of them
comes back here, I know,
they've got better sense:

just the crazy poet
well hooked on the past,
a sucker for memories.


## POMEGRANATES IN STUDIO ONE


In the TV studio the poet
has begun to read his poem
"The Pomegranates,"
a good one, he hasn't written
too many better.
            But someone
has placed four real (live?) pomegranates
in a bowl, and beside it another bowl
in which two more of the fruit
have been halved and quartered,
the whole thing sitting on a table now
with spotlights and cameras
on it.
        Strange how the eyes
cut off the words my ears strain to hear,
eyes pulling me away
from the poem and the poet,
all because of this radiant, natural fact.

Is it because we are tired
of too many words, even good ones,
or have we let the eyes
overpower the mind, leaving eyes
too undisciplined?
                    While I ponder this
and a poet exclaims on about pomegranates,
the whole barn of a building glows
from those fruited halves, those quarters,
blood-red on a table. . . .


## THE END OF SUMMER


Frenzied whine
of cicada's bandsaw
is silent now.

Only wood uncut
that branch he's fastened to.

# THE PEN-AND-INK CLERKS

No need for anyone
to phase us out – we'll arrange it ourselves
by death, disillusionment and drink,
roughly in that order.
                    But only the luckiest die,
and failure's a slow-eating process (like acid
it takes time to do its work). Drink on the other hand
is a luxury most of us can't afford
to get trapped in; those who do
live on with a double nightmare.

But while we last
we try to give our best, pride and habit
being two things that die hard with us.
Do we feel a great bitterness?
I think not. Fear is what we feel most,
whether we admit it or not. Fear for the future,
fear of the machines that the slick ones
told us at first would work with us,
work for us. Now we see them growing
slowly into masters, into monsters,
and we the slaves. And all done so skilfully
we were hardly aware of it happening
before it was much too late. So we fear them.
But it's done, it's over.
We work now from day to day
with our eyes always straining harder
under dim lighting we never noticed
even five years ago. Our pen and ink slides
across our record books, our ledgers,
and sometimes we imagine for a moment
nothing has changed, that it's the same as before,
as back in the good old days.
No harm in that, dreams are still allowed.

# MIRIAM WADDINGTON

## HOW EACH ONE BECOMES ANOTHER
## IN THE EARLY WORLD

speak me
my images
your words
are earlier
they shout
in the morning
when I am
still asleep

slow to wake
at noon I hear
your voice
speaking my
images   I wake
but I am not
me   I am you
speaking my
images and

my words are
earlier   they
shout in the
morning   they
wake everyone
who is slow
to wake and
now I am you

speaking my
images and the
slow to wake
are all awake
they go out
in the world
they are not
afraid of

being awake
not afraid
of speaking
their images
in words that
are earlier
newer than
now    louder
than morning

# TRANSITION

I am asleep
somewhere above
    the wind
loveblind   I dream
of pure
    nothing
the sky hangs
    over the cold
islands   the hills are
    weatherless
I am lying
    in a new cradle
of visibility
    the faraway telescope
of home

# LOVE POEM

I will swallow your
eyes and leave only
pools of darkness.

I will take the words
from your mouth and leave
only lakes of stillness.

Attend to my miracle,
I am kissing your body
making it white as stone,

The pools and lakes
of your eyes and mouth,
the white stone

Of your body will
make a labyrinth
of fabled cities,

And a marbled palace
of many rooms where
the whole world

Will be glad to pay
admission to wander
through the many rooms,

To look at my
miracle pools and soft
monuments until

At last the whole world
will go to sleep happy
at eight o'clock

Under a soft white fleece.

# THE NINETEEN THIRTIES ARE OVER

The nineteen thirties
are over; we survived
the depression, the Sacco-
Vanzetti of childhood
saw Tom Mooney smiling
at us from photographs,
put a rose on the grave
of Eugene Debs, listened
to our father's stories
of the Winnipeg strike and
joined the study groups
of the OBU always keeping
one eye on the revolution.

Later we played records
with thorn needles, Josh
White's *Talking Union* and
Prokofief's *Lieutenant Kije,*
shuddered at the sound of
bells and all those wolves
whirling past us in snow
on the corner of Portage
and Main, but in my mind
summer never ended on the
shores of Gimli where we
looked across to an Icelandic
paradise we could never see
the other side of; and I
dreamed of Mexico and shining
birds who beckoned to me
from the gold-braided lianas
of my own wonder.

These days I step out
from the frame of my wind-
battered house into Toronto
city; somewhere I still
celebrate sunlight, touch
the rose on the grave of
Eugene Debs but I walk
carefully in this land
of sooty snow; I pass the
rich houses and double
garages and I am not really
this middle-aged professor
but someone from
Winnipeg whose bones ache
with the broken revolutions
of Europe, and even now
I am standing on the heaving
ploughed-up field
of my father's old war.

## WIVES' TALES

When I married
my English
husband my Jewish
father said:
he'll get drunk
come home and
beat you,
you'll starve or
feed on green
pork stew –
well he didn't
and I didn't.

And my mother
being more
practical said:
if at least he
was a professor –
well he wasn't
and I was or
became.

Furthermore,
my mother said,
with a marriage
like that it's
plain curtains
for simple
you –

Well it was
curtains
in a way for a
while for me;
but for him
it was curtains
too and for him
forever and for
always.

# THE POETS

**MILTON ACORN** (born in Charlottetown, 1923)

When his book, *I've Tasted My Blood,* failed to win the Governor General's Award for 1969, a number of poets presented him with a prize of their own, calling him "The People's Poet." He was given the Governor General's Award for 1975 (*The Island Means Minago*).

**MARGARET ATWOOD** (born in Ottawa, 1939)

Winner of the Governor General's Award for 1966 (*The Circle Game*), she has published three novels, *The Edible Woman, Surfacing,* and *Lady Oracle* , and a thematic guide to Canadian literature, *Survival.*

**MARGARET AVISON** (born in Galt, Ontario, 1918)

Her childhood was spent in the West. Her pre-Christian publications included a history book for children, a social work survey, a ghost-written biography, and *Winter Sun,* which received the Governor General's Award for 1960.

**EARLE BIRNEY** (born in Calgary, 1904)

Winner of the Governor General's Award for 1942 *(David and Other Poems)* and 1945 *(Now Is Time),* he has written two novels, *Turvey,* re-issued in an unexpurgated version in 1976, and *Down the Long Table.* His most recent book of poems is *The Rugging & the Morning Times. The Cow Jumped over the Moon* is an account of the writing of some of his poems.

**GEORGE BOWERING** (born in Penticton, B.C., 1935)

He has produced poetry, fiction, criticism, and broadcast journalism. A novel *(Mirror on the Floor)* was published in 1967. He won the Governor General's Award for 1969 *(Rocky Mount Foot* and *The Gangs of Cosmos).*

**LEONARD COHEN** (born in Montreal, 1934)

His novels are *The Favourite Game* and *Beautiful Losers.* He declined the Governor General's Award for 1968 to his *Selected Poems.* He has had a considerable career as a popular composer-entertainer.

**LOUIS DUDEK** (born in Montreal, 1918)

For ten years he was editor of *Delta* magazine, and he has been editor of the publishing groups Delta Canada and DC books. His works include criticism, a history of publishing *(Literature and the Press)* and some dozen books of poetry.

**JOHN GLASSCO** (born in Montreal, 1909)

He has made statements as a poet, novelist, memoirist, pornographer, editor, and translator. His brilliant *Memoirs of Montparnasse* was published in 1970. His *Selected Poems* won the Governor General's Award for 1971.

**PHYLLIS GOTLIEB** (born in Toronto, 1926)

She has written verse drama, science fiction, and poetry. A novel *(Why Should I Have All The Grief?)* was published in 1969. Her latest science fiction novel is *O Master Caliban!*

**RALPH GUSTAFSON** (born near Sherbrooke, Quebec, 1909)

He has edited several anthologies of Canadian poetry for Penguin books, and is a broadcaster on music for the CBC. The Governor General's Award for 1974 was given to his *Fire on Stone,* which also won the A. J. M. Smith Award of Michigan State University.

**DAVID HELWIG** (born in Toronto, 1938)

He has been a consulting editor for Oberon Press, literary manager for CBC television drama and script editor for a CBC television police series. He has written both fiction and plays.

**GEORGE JOHNSTON** (born in Hamilton, Ontario, 1913)

His studies in Old Norse have resulted in splendid translations of *The Saga of Gisli, The Faroe Islanders' Saga,* and *The Greenlanders' Saga.*

**A. M. KLEIN** (born in Montreal, 1909; died, 1972)

He was given a Governor General's Award in 1941 for *The Rocking Chair and Other Poems.* His *The Second Scroll* deals with a spiritual pilgrimage to the Promised Land.

**IRVING LAYTON** (born near Bucharest, Rumania, 1912)

*A Red Carpet for the Sun* won the Governor General's Award for 1959. His poems and opinions continue to astonish and delight many and to infuriate some. His collected prose was published as a volume called *Engagements*.

**DENNIS LEE** (born in Toronto, 1939)

*Civil Elegies* won a Governor General's Award for 1972. He has published two popular books of poetry for children, *Alligator Pie* and *Nicholas Knock and Other Poems*.

**DOROTHY LIVESAY** (born in Winnipeg, 1909)

Two of her books have won Governor General's Awards, *Day and Night* (1944) and *Poems for People* (1947). She has edited the anthology, *Forty Women Poets of Canada*.

**GWENDOLYN MacEWEN** (born in Toronto, 1941)

*The Shadow Maker* won a Governor General's Award for 1969. She has published two novels, *Julian the Magician* and *King of Egypt, King of Dreams*, and a book of stories, *Noman*.

**JAY MacPHERSON** (born in London, England, 1931)

*The Boatman* won the Governor General's Award for 1957. She has written a prose work for young readers called *Four Ages of Man*. She teaches English at Victoria College, University of Toronto.

**ELI MANDEL** (born in Estevan, Saskatchewan, 1922)

*An Idiot Joy* was given a Governor General's Award for 1967. He has edited *Poets of Contemporary Canada 1960-1970* and *Contexts of Canadian Criticism*.

**B. P. NICHOL** (born in Vancouver, 1944)

bp Nichol (the usage he prefers) is a leading practitioner of sound and concrete poetry. His *The True Eventual Story of Billy the Kid* won a Governor General's Award for 1970.

**JOHN NEWLOVE** (born in Regina, 1938)

His *Lies* received a Governor General's Award for 1972. He has been a publisher's editor and a writer-in-residence at three universities.

**ALDEN NOWLAN** (born near Windsor, Nova Scotia, 1933)

He received a Governor General's Award for *Bread, Wine and Salt* (1967). He has published a novel, *Various Persons Named Kevin O'Brien,* and a collection of stories, *Miracle at Indian River.* A play, *Frankenstein, the Man Who Became God,* was written in collaboration with Walter Learning.

**MICHAEL ONDAATJE** (born in Ceylon, 1943)

*The Collected Works of Billy the Kid* won a Governor General's Award for 1970. He has made two documentary films, *Sons of Captain Poetry* (on bp nicol) and *The Clinton Special* (on Theatre Passe Muraille's "Farm Show").

**P. K. PAGE** (born in Swanage, England, 1916)

*The Metal and the Flower* won the Governor General's Award for 1954. She has published a novel, *The Sun and the Moon,* stories, radio plays, and essays. As P. K. Irwin, she is a noted visual artist.

**AL PURDY** (born in Wooller, Ontario, 1918)

His *The Cariboo Horses* was given the Governor General's Award for 1965. He has written stories, essays, and radio and television plays, and has edited a number of anthologies, including the *Storm Warning* series of works by newer poets.

**JAMES REANEY** (born near Stratford, Ontario, 1926)

He has won the Governor General's Award three times: for *The Red Heart* (poetry, 1949); *A Suit of Nettles* (poetry, 1958); and *Twelve Letters to a Small Town* and *The Killdeer and Other Plays* (poetry and drama, 1962). He is a noted playwright.

**F. R. SCOTT** (born at St. Matthew's Rectory, Quebec, 1899)

Son of the poet Archdeacon F. G. Scott, he has been active in socialist politics (the CCF party) and, as a lawyer, in civil rights cases. He has published translations of French Canadian poetry.

**A. J. M. SMITH** (born in Montreal, 1902)

He is a well-known critic and anthologist. On leave from Michigan State University, he has taught at many Canadian universities, including Toronto, Queen's, Dalhousie, McGill, and Sir George Williams.

**RAYMOND SOUSTER** (born in Toronto, 1921)

*The Colour of the Times* won the Governor General's Award for 1964. He served in the RCAF during the Second World War. He has edited a number of anthologies.

**MIRIAM WADDINGTON** (born in Winnipeg, 1917)

She has edited *John Sutherland: Essays, Controversies, Poems* and *The Collected Poems of A.M. Klein* and is the author of a critical study, *A.M. Klein.* She contributed the poems in the National Film Board book, *Call Them Canadians.*

# SELECTED BIBLIOGRAPHY

Acorn, Milton. *I've Tasted My Blood.* McGraw-Hill Ryerson, 1969.
———. *More Poems for People.* NC Press, 1972.
———. *The Island Means Minago.* NC Press, 1975.

Atwood, Margaret. *The Circle Game.* Anansi, 1966.
———. *The Animals in that Country.* Oxford, 1968.
———. *Procedures for Underground.* Oxford, 1970.
———. *Power Politics.* Anansi, 1971.
———. *You Are Happy.* Oxford, 1974.
———. *Selected Poems.* Oxford, 1976.

Avison, Margaret. *Winter Sun.* University of Toronto, 1960.
———. *The Dumbfounding.* McLeod, 1966.

Birney, Earle. *Collected Poems,* Volumes I & II. McClelland and
    Stewart, 1975.

Bowering, George. *Touch, Selected Poems 1960-1970.* McClelland and
    Stewart, 1971.
———. *In the Flesh.* McClelland and Stewart, 1974.
———. *The Catch.* McClelland and Stewart, 1976.

Cohen, Leonard. *Selected Poems 1956-1968.* McClelland and Stewart,
    1968.
———. *The Energy of Slaves.* McClelland and Stewart, 1972.

Dudek, Louis. *Collected Poetry.* Delta Canada, 1971.

Glassco, John. *Selected Poems.* Oxford, 1971.

Gotlieb, Phyllis. *Within the Zodiac.* McClelland and Stewart, 1964.
———. *Ordinary, Moving.* Oxford, 1969.
———. *Doctor Umlaut's Earthly Kingdom.* Calliope Press, 1976.

Gustafson, Ralph. *Selected Poems.* McClelland and Stewart, 1972.
———. *Fire on Stone.* McClelland and Stewart, 1974.

Helwig, David. *The Sign of the Gunman.* Oberon, 1969.
_____. *The Best Name of Silence.* Oberon, 1972.

Johnston, George. *Happy Enough: Poems 1935-1970.* Oxford, 1972.

Klein, A. M. *The Collected Poems of A. M. Klein.* McGraw-Hill Ryerson, 1974.

Layton, Irving. *The Darkening Fire, Selected Poems 1945-1968.* McClelland and Stewart, 1975.
_____. *The Unwavering Eye, Selected Poems 1969-1975.* McClelland and Stewart, 1975.
_____. *For My Brother Jesus.* McClelland and Stewart, 1976.

Lee, Dennis. *Civil Elegies.* Anansi, 1972.

Livesay, Dorothy. *Collected Poems: The Two Seasons.* McGraw-Hill Ryerson, 1972.
_____. *Ice Age.* Press Porcépic, 1975.

MacEwen, Gwendolyn. *Magic Animals.* Macmillan, 1974.
_____. *The Fire-Eaters.* Oberon, 1976.

Macpherson, Jay. *The Boatman.* Oxford, 1957.
_____. *Welcoming Disaster.* Saannes, 1975.

Mandel, Eli. *Crusoe.* Anansi, 1973.

Newlove, John. *Black Night Window.* McClelland and Stewart, 1968.
_____. *The Cave.* McClelland and Stewart, 1970.
_____. *Lies.* McClelland and Stewart, 1972.

Nichol, B. P. *The True Eventual Story of Billy the Kid.* Weed/flower Press, 1970.
_____. *love a book of remembrances.* Talonbooks, 1974.

Nowlan, Alden. *Bread, Wine and Salt.* Clarke Irwin, 1967.
_____. *The Mysterious Naked Man.* Clarke Irwin, 1969.
_____. *Between Tears and Laughter.* Clarke Irwin, 1971.
_____. *I'm a Stranger Here Myself.* Clarke Irwin, 1974.

Ondaatje, Michael. *The Collected Works of Billy the Kid.*
Anansi, 1970.
————. *Rat Jelly.* Coach House Press, 1973.

Page, P.K. *Poems Selected and New.* Anansi, 1974.

Purdy, Al. *Selected.* McClelland and Stewart, 1972.
————. *Sex & Death.* McClelland and Stewart, 1973.
————. *Sundance at Dusk.* McClelland and Stewart, 1976.

Reaney, James. *Poems.* New Press, 1972.

Scott, F. R. *Selected Poems.* Oxford, 1966.
————. *The Dance Is One.* McClelland and Stewart, 1973.

Smith, A. J. M. *Poems New and Collected.* Oxford, 1967.

Souster, Raymond. *Selected Poems.* Oberon, 1972.
————. *Change-up.* Oberon, 1974.

Waddington, Miriam. *Say Yes.* Oxford, 1969.
————. *Driving Home.* Oxford, 1972.
————. *The Price of Gold.* Oxford, 1976.

# ACKNOWLEDGEMENTS

The publishers gratefully acknowledge the permission granted by copyright holders to reprint the poems in this volume:

MILTON ACORN

"In Memory of Tommy," "The Island," and "Sky's Poem for Christmas," from *I've Tasted My Blood*; and "Ho Chi Minh," "Riding With Joe Hensby," and "Bethuniverse," from *More Poems for the People*, reprinted by permission of the author.

MARGARET ATWOOD

"Journey to the Interior" and "The Settlers," from *The Circle Game*; and "They Eat Out" and "You Refuse to Own," from *Power Politics*, reprinted by permission of House of Anansi Press Limited.

"The Animals in that Country" and "Chronology," from *The Animals in that Country*; and "Procedures for Underground" and "Dreams of the Animals," from *Procedures for Underground*, reprinted by permission of Oxford University Press.

"There is Only One of Everything," from *You Are Happy*, reprinted by permission of the author.

MARGARET AVISON

"Jonathan, o Jonathan," "Watershed," and "September Street," from *Winter Sun*; and "Twilight," "July Man," "Words," "The Absorbed," "Miniature Biography," "Five Breaks," "The Dumbfounding," "In Eporphyrial Harness," and "Natural/Unnatural," from *The Dumbfounding*, reprinted by permission of the author.

EARLE BIRNEY

"This Page My Pigeon," "Atlantic Door," "From the Hazel Bough," "She Is," "Bushed," and "El Greco: *Espolio*," from *Collected Poems*, Vol. I; and "Irapuato," "The Bear on the Delhi Road," "Caribbean Kingdoms," "For George Lamming," and "Hokkai in the Dew Line Snows," from *Collected Poems*, Vol. II, reprinted with permission of The Canadian Publishers, McClelland and Stewart Limited, Toronto.

DAVID HELWIG

"Late October," "Return," and "Imaginary Evening, Real Dark," from *The Sign of the Gunman;* and "Vision" and "Drunken Poem," from *The Best Name of Silence,* reprinted by permission of Oberon Press.

GEORGE JOHNSTON

"Love of the City," "Money in Pocket," "Spring Moon," "Us Together," "Indoors," and "Nonstop Jetflight to Halifax," from *Happy Enough,* reprinted by permission of Oxford University Press.
  "War on the Periphery," reprinted by permission, © 1951 The New Yorker Magazine Inc.

A.M. KLEIN

"Sweet Singer," "Job Reviles," "Simeon Takes Hints from His Environs," "Once in a Year," "Psalm XXXVI: A Psalm Touching Genealogy," "And in that Drowning Instant," "Meditation upon Survival," "Political Meeting," "Lookout: Mount Royal," and "Stance of the Amidah," from *The Collected Poems of A.M. Klein,* compiled by Miriam Waddington, © 1974. Reprinted by permission of McGraw-Hill Ryerson Limited.

IRVING LAYTON

"The Black Huntsmen," "Death of Moishe Lazarovitch," "Seven O'Clock Lecture," "Golfers," "Cat Dying in Autumn," and "For Musia's Grandchildren," from *The Darkening Fire;* "The Haunting," "End of the White Mouse," "Osip Mandelshtam," and "Terrorists," from *The Unwavering Eye;* and "Saint Pinchas," from *For My Brother Jesus,* reprinted by permission of The Canadian Publishers, McClelland and Stewart Limited, Toronto.

DENNIS LEE

"400: Coming Home," "Thursday," and "Civil Elegy 5," from *Civil Elegies,* reprinted by permission of House of Anansi Press Limited.
  "1838," from *Nicholas Knock and Other People,* ©Dennis Lee, reprinted by permission of The Macmillan Company of Canada Limited.

## ALDEN NOWLAN

"I, Icarus," "The Spy," "The Changeling," "The Dark Companions," "Revelation," and "A Boy in a Red Loin Cloth," from *Bread, Wine and Salt;* "X-Ray," "Re-Entry," "Five Days in Hospital," "A Black Plastic Button and a Yellow Yoyo," and "O'Sullivan's World," from *The Mysterious Naked Man;* "Cornflowers," and "Long Ago and Far Away," from *Between Tears and Laughter;* and "He Perceives That His Son Is Becoming a Man" and "Act Two," from *I'm a Stranger Here Myself,* reprinted by permission of Clarke, Irwin & Company Limited.

## MICHAEL ONDAATJE

"After shooting Gregory," "The street of the slow moving animals," and "The end of it," from *The Collected Works of Billy the Kid,* reprinted by permission of House of Anansi Press Limited.
   "Date" and "White Dwarfs," from *Rat Jelly;* and "Light," reprinted by permission of the author.

## P.K. PAGE

"Presentation," "The Landlady," "Little Girls," "The Knitters," "Man With One Small Hand," "Mineral," "Photos of a Salt Mine," "Element," "The Permanent Tourists," "They Might Have Been Zebras," and "The Murder," from *Poems Selected and New,* reprinted by permission of House of Anansi Press Limited.

## AL PURDY

"The Cariboo Horses," "Percy Lawson," "Arctic Rhododendrons," "Poem," "Poem for One of the Annettes," "Roblin's Mills (2)," and "The Country North of Belleville," from *Selected;* and "Depression in Namu, B.C." and "Tourist Itinerary," from *Sex & Death,* reprinted by permission of The Canadian Publishers, McClelland and Stewart Limited, Toronto.

## JAMES REANEY

"Mrs. Wentworth," "The Red Heart," "The Royal Visit," "The Upper Canadian," "The Katzenjammer Kids," "The Hummingbird," "The Morning Dew," "First Letter," and "Sixth Letter," reprinted from *Poems,* James Reaney, New Press, Toronto. Copyright © 1972 by James Reaney.

## F. R. SCOTT

"Trans Canada," "To Certain Friends," and "A Grain of Rice," from *Selected Poems;* and "On Saying Good-Bye to My Room in Chancellor Day Hall," "Dancing," and "Mackenzie River," from *The Dance Is One,* reprinted by permission of the author.

## A.J.M. SMITH

"Field of Long Grass," "The Sorcerer," "Resurrection of Arp," "News of the Phoenix," "The Widsom of Old Jelly Roll," and "Far West," from *Poems New and Collected,* reprinted by permission of Oxford University Press.

## RAYMOND SOUSTER

"Jeannette" and "Armadale Avenue Revisited," from *The Colour of the Times/Ten Elephants on Yonge Street,* reprinted by permission of McGraw-Hill Ryerson Limited.

"The Launching," "Easter Sunday," "Pomegranates In Studio One," and "The End of Summer," from *Selected Poems;* and "The Pen-and-Ink Clerks," from *Change-up,* reprinted by permission of Oberon Press.

## MIRIAM WADDINGTON

"How Each One Becomes Another in the Early World" and "Transition," from *Say Yes;* and "Wives' Tales" from *The Price of Gold,* reprinted by permission of the author.

"The Nineteen Thirties are Over" and "Love Poem," from *Driving Home,* reprinted by permission of Oxford University Press.